SOLD OUT TWO-GETHER

SOLD OUT
TWO-GETHER

Bill McCartney

Lyndi McCartney

Connie Neal

WORD PUBLISHING
NASHVILLE
A Thomas Nelson Company

Published by Word Publishing
Nashville, TN

Published in association with Sealy M. Yates, Literary Agent, Orange, California.

Library of Congress Cataloging-in-Publication Data

McCartney, Bill.
    Sold out—two-gether: a couples workbook / by William McCartney, Lyndi McCartney, Connie Neal.
      p. cm.
    ISBN 0-8499-4046-X
    1. Spouses—Religious life. 2. Marriage—Religious aspects—Christianity. I. McCartney, Lyndi, 1962–   . II. Neal, C. W. (Connie W.), 1958–   . III. Title.
    BV4596.M3M43 1999
    248.8′44—dc21

             98–54740
             CIP

Printed in the United States of America
99 00 01 02 03 04 QPV 9 8 7 6 5 4 3 2 1

Contents

Introduction

It's Not What You Might Expect

Sold Out Two-Gether is not what you might expect.

It's Not a Study Guide for *Sold Out*

While this is a sequel to Bill McCartney's *Sold Out*, it is not a study guide for that book. In *Sold Out* Bill chronicled his spiritual journey—how he went from being sold out to his childhood values and dreams, to his career in coaching football, to his personal relationship with Jesus Christ, to his involvement with Promise Keepers. He wondered throughout that book whether he was selling out his family while being sold out to other interests. Bill also chronicled what it means to be 100 percent sold out to God, completely committed, "on fire" with a white-hot passion for the things of God. He taught about the spiritual disciplines he believes are essential for a "sold out" relationship with God, things like worshiping, praying, getting into God's Word, engaging in spiritual warfare.

As Bill wrote *Sold Out*, he felt led of the Lord to include his wife, Lyndi's, perspective on what he was chronicling. Lyndi's counterpoint essays were included in that book. Her essays were written with the help of Connie Neal. Thus the collaboration that continues in this workbook was born. What Bill saw from including Lyndi's perspective was that while he was passionately living his life, devoting himself to his career, his faith, and even his ministry, something was missing. The process of looking over the whole of his life and beliefs beside Lyndi's reflections on the same life they shared brought him to a startling conclusion.

All that he devoted himself to was basically good, but it rang hollow when he realized that he and his wife had often lived side by side but alone when God wanted them to share the spiritual life he had called them into as spiritual partners.

This workbook is the response to that realization. It is an attempt to begin doing what Bill and Lyndi discovered they—and all Christian married couples—need to do in order to live as equal spiritual partners 100 percent sold out to God together.

It's Not a Marriage Improvement Workbook

You might expect *Sold Out Two-Gether* to teach you how to improve your marriage. While your marriage will probably improve by doing this workbook with your mate, this is not about how to improve your marriage or fix problems in your relationship. Bill and Lyndi don't pretend to be marriage experts.

What It Is

This is a spiritual growth workbook designed to be used by a husband and wife together. In these pages we have taken all the elements that Bill identified in *Sold Out* as being vital to a passionate love relationship with God and designed them to be pursued by a husband and wife together as equal spiritual partners. When you do this with your mate, you may experience wonderful benefits to your marriage, but the focus here is on building relationship with God, obeying God, and fulfilling God's purposes for your lives, your family, your church, and the world—and doing it together. The marital benefits are an additional blessing!

How It Works

Each week will start off with a general introduction by Connie Neal. Bill McCartney will offer a message to the husband and Lyndi McCartney will offer a message to the wife. Then you will find five days' worth of exercises to do together. The power of this workbook will not reach you if you just read it; you've got to *do* it to get the benefits. It will only work in your life if the two of you work through it together.

In order to accommodate a variety of schedules, we designed this workbook so you can adapt it to your lifestyle. While becoming sold out to God together requires commitment, you can craft that commitment to fit the realities of your schedule. We offer the following suggestions for various situations.

If You Have Plenty of Time and Want to Finish in Eight Weeks
Set aside enough time each day to do the entire day's readings and exercises together.

If You Want to Finish in Eight Weeks but Are Pressed for Time
You can do an abbreviated version of the exercises. Each day, read the purpose and premise sections together. In the practice section, focus on the items marked with a ⏳. Then close by reading the promises and praying together. If you want to come back later to go deeper, you can revisit the practice sections and do the parts you skipped. Some days you will find everything marked with an icon. That means all parts of the practice are essential.

If You Are Pressed for Time and Don't Mind Taking Sixteen Weeks
Allow yourself two weeks to complete each week's material. Break each day's material into two parts. Take one day to read the purpose and premise sections, then preview the practice section. The following day, do the practice, promises, and prayer sections. By dividing the material in half, you afford yourselves time to think about the scriptural principles to be applied before you work through them together. This has the added benefit of allowing for a more thoughtful response.

WEEK ONE

Commit Yourselves to Seek First
the Kingdom of God Together

Introduction

From the outset, let us assure you that we will encourage the two of you to become 100 percent sold out to God—together. You're already expressing such a desire by using this workbook. Bear in mind that your success and enjoyment here depend on each of you entering into this commitment freely and with enthusiasm.

The exercises that follow are not designed to teach you new things but to have you respond to things you probably already know—and to do so together. We pray you will yield to God's will as revealed in the Holy Bible and be filled afresh with the power of the Holy Spirit, so you can walk in closer fellowship with Jesus Christ and each other.

You start during this first week by rightly connecting with each other and God. In this way, you will not only lend your human strengths and helpfulness to each other's spiritual growth, but you will also become a conduit through which the life of Jesus Christ can flow to touch each other's lives. Being rightly connected to God and each other makes a way for God to flow through you as a couple to impact your family, church, community, and world to the glory of God.

All of this begins as you commit yourselves to seek first the kingdom of God together. Each day this week you will consider aspects of committing yourselves wholeheartedly to God and various ways of connecting with each other: connecting spiritually, intertwining your everyday lives with each other and God, and recommitting yourselves to your marriage vows.

Man to Man
with Bill McCartney

In these pages you will be asked to make a commitment. This is no small thing. In fact, making and keeping a commitment is a solemn act before a holy God. Almighty God is a covenant-keeping God; he always keeps his promises. He also calls us into covenant with himself and to keep our covenant with our mate. According to Webster, a covenant is "a formal, binding agreement." There's no room for hedging on this kind of contract. It's absolute! If one side breaks it, that side is often subject to severe penalties.

As Moses told the leaders of Israel regarding covenants in Numbers 30:1–2, "This is what the Lord commands: When a man makes a vow to the Lord or takes an oath to obligate himself by a pledge, he must not break his word but must do everything he said." In other words, whatever we promise or swear to do, God *commands* that we follow through. It's not a request. It's a demand.

Joshua was one of those who heard Moses' statement and took it to heart. When he was conquering city after city in the land of Canaan, the Gibeonites disguised themselves to appear as visitors from a faraway land and made a treaty with Israel. Joshua forgot to pray beforehand and didn't find out that he had been deceived until later. But it didn't matter. *He* had entered into a covenant with them and was bound to honor it fully. This meant that when the Gibeonites were threatened with war, the Israelites were even obligated to risk their lives to aid them in battle!

It was at this particular time, when the Israelites were defending the Gibeonites, that Joshua asked God to stop the sun and the moon in the sky to enable them to defeat the enemy. Even though the covenant had been entered into deceitfully, God honored Joshua for keeping it, answering his prayer and stopping the sun in its tracks for a whole day (Josh. 9:10–15). God will literally move heaven and earth for those who keep their promises!

On the other hand, four hundred years later when King Saul ignored the treaty and went to war against the Gibeonites, thinking he was doing the right thing, the Lord punished Israel with three years of famine (2 Sam. 21).

God honors and shows himself strong on behalf of those who keep their promises but doles out severe consequences to those who don't. This is especially true when we make vows before him—like our wedding vows. The Lord expects us to keep *all* of the vows, promises, and covenants we make, whether they are with him or with other people.

For men who call themselves Promise Keepers, keeping promises in not an option. It's an *absolute* necessity! As those who possess the mind of Christ, we need to think about keeping our promises in the strongest of terms. We serve a covenant-keeping God who calls us into covenant with himself. And he expects us—he commands us—to be covenant-keeping men.

As married men, we are in a permanent and indissoluble union. God has made us "one flesh" with our wife. Week one serves as a refresher for this unique God-inspired relationship. Marital maturity is our mission within the greater mission of seeking first the kingdom of God and his righteousness. Let's move out to accomplish both and advance the kingdom of God.

Woman to Woman
with Lyndi McCartney

In *Sold Out* I shared how a friend taught me what she and her husband had learned in premarital counseling. The pastor had told them that a marriage relationship could be envisioned as a triangle with three equal sides: one side flat on the ground with two sides pointing toward the pinnacle. She drew the triangle with a dot, representing God—who could be conceived as being at the pinnacle—

at the top. She then drew two dots—one on each side—explaining that these represented each marriage partner's life. Then she drew two dots closer to the pinnacle, explaining that if each person focused on moving closer to God—individually—each would simultaneously draw closer to the other while growing closer to God. That impacted my thought process drastically. I can follow directions, but if I can't see what is going on, the directions may not make sense to me. I believed that Bill, being the head of the household, should straighten up and fly right; then I could. My oh my, what a difference a triangle makes! Seeing how growing closer to the Lord individually would simultaneously draw us closer stoked my fires of passion. That's what I always wanted; I just had the triangle tilted sideways. I had put Bill at the pinnacle, and the Lord and I were trying to grow closer to him. I'm telling you, that just doesn't work.

I believe the secret to life and the secret to true love is found in this first part. It may only take you a week to work through it, but you'll begin a process that goes on for a lifetime. No matter where you think you are in your faith, study and apply yourself to this chapter as if your heart were hearing it for the first time. Deepen your connection with the Lord and free your heart to love.

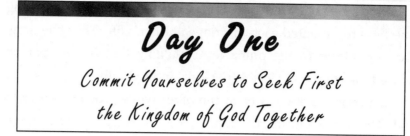

Day One

Commit Yourselves to Seek First
the Kingdom of God Together

Purpose

- To understand what it means to seek first God's kingdom

- To commit yourselves afresh to seek first the kingdom of God

- To complete this workbook together in the next eight weeks

Premise

Jesus calls all who would follow him to put him first in their lives. This is a matter of free will and an individual decision, even though you are doing it together. The Gospel of Matthew says that crowds flocked to Jesus. People said they wanted to follow Jesus, but many had other things to do first. One said to him, "Lord, first let me go and bury my father." But Jesus told him, "Follow me, and let the dead bury their own dead" (Matt. 8:21–22). There were the crowds, then the disciples, then those disciples who were willing to put following Jesus ahead of all other earthly pursuits or obligations. Those who put Jesus first are sold out to God.

Luke records a similar account about people who said they wanted to follow Jesus, *but. . . .* They wanted to follow Jesus *but* had something else to do first. Most people have obstacles that stand between them and being 100 percent sold out to God. Honestly consider what presents an obstacle for you. Consider how you might complete this statement, "Jesus I want to follow you, but . . ." Briefly share with each other how you would complete this statement. And remember, speak for yourself not your partner.

What It Means to Seek First the Kingdom of God
Your commitment to seek first the kingdom of God involves pledging allegiance

to God as the rightful king of your life. It includes recognizing the Bible—God's Holy Word—as the arbiter of truth and righteousness in life by which you measure your behavior, beliefs, and attitudes. It involves yielding your will to God so that you become willing to do God's bidding on earth as it is in heaven.

Here are some questions to help you gauge where you are in right relation to the kingdom of God as you begin this workbook.

1. Are you willing to acknowledge God as king over your life? Circle one: Yes / No / Not Sure

2. Are you willing to accept the Bible as God's inspired Word and use it as the standard by which you measure all your behavior, beliefs, and attitudes? Circle one: Yes / No / Not Sure

3. Are you willing to note and acknowledge whenever your will (what you want to do) differs from God's (what God's Word says to do)? Circle one: Yes / No / Not Sure

4. Are you willing to seek first God's kingdom and his righteousness? Circle one: Yes / No / Not Sure

Notice that the questions begin *are you willing;* if you are willing, God can make you able. If you are willing to acknowledge God as king and the Holy Bible as your standard for life, if you are willing to acknowledge to each other whenever your will differs from God's, you are well on your way to becoming sold out to God.

You will not always agree with each other as you go through this process, and that is fine. What matters most is that you agree about what settles disagreements in God's kingdom. It's not a matter of what either of you says or the force with which you say it. What matters is what God's Word says. As you examine your lives together in this light, you will see areas where you fall short of God's will. Don't let that cause you to turn back or get discouraged. Remember, in God's kingdom, he provides not only the standard of righteousness but also the means of attaining righteousness. When we enter God's kingdom, we do so by *receiving* the righteousness of Jesus Christ by faith. Then we are empowered to live rightly by the Holy Spirit within us.

This is part of the premise upon which we'll build to put God's will into practice in our daily life.

Practice

The first step is to make sure you are in God's kingdom and have received his righteousness. In God's kingdom, you do not earn righteousness by how well you live. Rather, how well you live will result from understanding that your righteousness is a free gift and receiving that gift from God. Let's do that now.

Read Romans 5:8–21 together and answer the following questions.

1. How are we saved from God's wrath—by being good enough or by receiving Jesus? _____

2. How does one obtain righteousness? Is it by behaving righteously most of the time or by receiving God's gift of righteousness made available through Jesus Christ? _____

3. If you were seeking eternal life in God's kingdom, would you do so by (A) trying your hardest to be righteous in your own strength or (B) accepting the grace of God that gives us eternal life through Jesus Christ our Lord? Circle one: A / B

⏳ 4. Have you each received God's gift of righteousness that brings eternal life by trusting Jesus Christ as your Savior? Circle one: Yes / No / Not Sure

Briefly share with each other when you made your decision to receive Christ and how it happened. If you're not sure, or have not received this free gift of righteousness and eternal life, you can do so now. You do this by believing that Jesus Christ is the only begotten Son of God, that he died to pay for all of your sins, that he rose from the dead, and that his blood was full payment for your sins. If you are willing to receive Jesus Christ as your Savior and enter God's kingdom, pray the prayer in the box with your mate. Then talk to your local pastor about your conversion and being baptized.

⏳ Entering God's Kingdom

Our Father in Heaven,

I want to receive the gift of righteousness you have offered us through Jesus Christ. I believe that Jesus is the only begotten Son of God, that he died to pay for all of my sins, that he rose from the dead, and that his blood can make me righteous in your eyes. Today I put my trust in him, believing that you will give me eternal life as you promised. Amen!

⧖ If this is the first time either of you have chosen to receive the gift of righteousness and eternal life through Jesus Christ, seek out and speak to a local pastor and get involved in a local church. Fellowship is an important way to grow in faith.

Once you are secure in your righteousness through faith in Jesus Christ, live in accordance with God's Word *by the power of the Holy Spirit.* This ongoing way of life will be upheld by the daily spiritual exercises in this workbook, which you will do together.

⧖ *Commit Yourselves to Completing This Workbook Together*
Your decision to work through this text together will involve a minimum commitment of thirty minutes per day, five days per week, for eight weeks. It will also involve a promise to listen to each other, to show respect for each other's perspective, and to complete the daily spiritual exercises together. Are you both willing to make such a commitment? Husband: _____ Wife: _____

⧖ *Set Aside the Time*
Completing this workbook will require you to set aside an appointed time to meet together to go through the material and do any of the spiritual exercises. Check both of your daily calendars for the next eight weeks and set aside times to consistently meet. You will benefit more if you can arrange these times so that if you find you want to take more than thirty minutes, you have some flexibility to do so.

⧖ *Make Your Commitment in Writing*
The following written commitment is the first step in doing what you have probably already decided to do. Read and sign it if you are willing:

We, _____ and _____, agree on _____ _____, of the year _____ to seek first the kingdom of God together. We agree to commit at least thirty minutes each day, for five days of each week, for the next eight weeks or until we complete this process. When we come together, we agree to give each other and the material our full attention.

We also agree to encourage and support each other in this endeavor. We will seek to build each other up rather than to tear each other down. We will submit ourselves, individually, to God's Word—to seek to live in accordance with God's will as revealed in the Bible, not just to learn about it. We agree to seek God for the help of the Holy Spirit so that we may do God's will by his power that works in us mightily.

Our appointed days each week will be (circle five): Monday / Tuesday / Wednesday / Thursday / Friday / Saturday / Sunday

Our appointed time to do this each day will be: _____

Signature: _____

Signature: _____

Promises

God's Promise to You
"But seek first his kingdom and his righteousness, and all these things will be given to you as well" (Matt. 6:33).

Your Promise to Each Other
To complete this workbook together.

Prayer

Our Father in heaven,

What a privilege it is to be invited into your kingdom. Lord, please help us keep the commitment we have made to you and each other. Please lead us and strengthen us as we commit ourselves afresh to seek first your kingdom and your righteousness. Amen!

Day Two
Tighten Your Connection with Each Other and God

Purpose

- To recognize and acknowledge that God has already joined you together

- To see how your lives can connect so God can flow through you together

- To assess where your union may have begun to loosen or disconnect

- To begin doing things to tighten your connection with each other and God

Premise

Those who are married don't need to try to *become* united. It is enough to recognize and acknowledge that God himself unites a man and woman as husband and wife when they enter into their marriage vows.

Jesus said of marriage, "At the beginning of creation God 'made them male and female. For this reason a man will leave his father and mother and be united to his wife, and the two will become one flesh.' So they are no longer two, but one. Therefore what God has joined together, let man not separate" (Mark 10:6–9).

In this passage, Jesus addressed the issue of divorce. While divorce is the complete severing of the marital union, there are other ways a marriage can disconnect. Today, you will consider how you can make sure you and your mate stay well connected.

The marital union can be likened to joining two segments of pipe to make a longer, unified piece for liquid to flow through. You could take two sections of pipe with male and female ends and twist them together, but they would be prone to leak under pressure. Or you could use copper pipes and solder the separate pieces into a fitting. This would assure a more secure and permanent union. When heat is applied to the copper pipes and fitting, the soldering compound melts to seal two pieces into the fitting. The two become one—united with the fitting through the soldering process.

The purpose of connecting pipes is to create a unit through which liquid can flow farther, forcefully, and without leaking. If you relied on twisting the male and female ends of threaded pipes together, the connection might loosen under the pressure of flowing liquid and could spray at the point where the pipes should be snugly joined. This would diminish the force of the flow—and create quite a mess. However, the soldered pipe union would not yield to such pressure.

Here's how this applies to marriage. God created us male and female with the intention that men and women would have the option of coming together in marriage—the two becoming one. Any man and woman willing to commit to each other in marriage can come together, without inviting God into the relationship. This is like the two pieces of pipe that can be twisted together. Just as this kind of union can become disconnected under pressure, a marriage held together merely by commitment to one another can become disconnected.

A more permanent marital union can be formed when God is at the center of the relationship and each marriage partner is devoted to God as well as to the other. God is like the fitting, fire, and solder that holds each of you in a marriage with a secure and permanent union. When God is at the center of your union, and the passionate love of God is the fire that unifies you, your marriage gains a strength beyond human commitment. With God as the fitting and the solder that holds the two of you together, your marriage will be able to withstand pressures you might not be able to withstand by relying only on your own human strength.

God is not only the center of your union, he is also the source and substance of what flows through your lives. God intends you to be conduits of his blessings to each other—conduits of the Holy Spirit, God's love, wisdom, power, grace, mercy, and so on. God wants you to come together in such a way that he can flow through you to fill needs in each other. He also wants to flow through your union to bless your family, church, community, and world.

When you connect spiritually, something happens that far transcends what either of you can do by just sharing yourselves. Neither of you has all that is necessary to fill your mate's needs. But if you are rightly connected to God and your mate, God can fill you and flow through you to help you meet each other's needs by the power of the Holy Spirit, which is not limited as are human resources.

When you see your marriage in this way, the question of which partner is "more spiritual" becomes irrelevant. The goal becomes offering all that you are to God and each other, then trusting to fill each person's needs. This can take pressure off whichever of you feels less "spiritual."

Practice

⧗ When husband and wife—even Christians—rely only on each other and their human connection in marriage, they risk having that connection loosen. When your connection with God and each other is not as tight as it should be, there will be noticeable signs of leaking and spewing in the relationship. Check to see if any of these signs are present in your marriage: (1) your godly influence in each other's life has dissipated, (2) the force of the love you once had for each other has diminished, (3) you have to deal with relational messes caused by spewing emotions or outbursts of anger, (4) you see evidence of an ongoing slow leak—little annoyances that you've opted not to deal with—that create a mess, or (5) one of you has shut off the flow of relationship between you, so very little real intimacy flows between you.

⧗ Which of the following statements describes your relationship? Be prepared to explain why without accusing your mate.

- We are married but somewhat disconnected. In many ways we're living separate lives.

- We're connected, but we're not as tight as we once were with each other.

- We are connected to each other, but I'm not sure our connection with each other includes God as much as it should.

- I feel like the more I try to connect to you, the more you disconnect.

- I sense that you are trying to connect with me, but I've been disconnecting from you.

- It seems like the flow—of God's Spirit, feelings, communication, sexual intimacy, shared desires, and hopes—has been cut off between us.

- I notice outbursts of emotion that dissipate the flow of God in our relationship.

- Our union is tight with each other and God. I sense God flowing to you through me and to me through you, and I see God ministering to others through us together.

Take turns gently telling each other what you chose and why. As your partner speaks, listen and try to understand rather than defend yourself. Remember, your goal is to identify where your relationship could use some tightening up. Instead of just trying to solve the problems between you, bring all these concerns to God. Ask him to unify your marriage in a way that will eliminate the signs of concern you have noted.

⧗ Add to the prayer that follows a list of specific requests for God's help in your relationship regarding every point either of you identified. Ask God to show you how each of you can cooperate with his overall purpose for your union.

Promises

God's Promise to You
"'And the two will become one flesh.' So they are no longer two, but one" (Mark 10:7–8).

Your Promise to Each Other
To make an effort to stay connected with each other.

Prayer

Our Father in heaven,

Thank you for the mystery of marriage and that we do not have to make ourselves one because you already did so when we took our vows. Please show us if we are doing or have done anything to disconnect or loosen our union. If so, show us what we can do to tighten our relationship.

Lord God, we need your covering to keep our relationship with each other tight. Please help us to honor you and bless each other, continually tightening our relationship with each other and you.

Lord, as we remain united, release the flow of your Holy Spirit, your love, wisdom, power, grace, and all that you are to flow through us to each other and, through us together, to others. Amen!

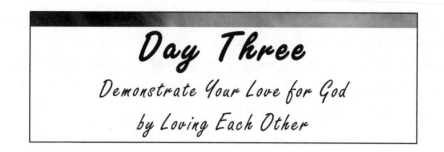

Day Three
Demonstrate Your Love for God by Loving Each Other

Purpose

- To understand the biblical connection between loving God and loving each other

- To change our minds and shift our spiritual focus, to demonstrate our love for God by how we love others—especially each other

- To actively demonstrate our love for God by loving people—especially each other

Premise

The Bible clearly tells us that we are to love the Lord our God with all our heart, soul, mind, and strength—what we might call being sold out to God. Read the following verses that state this core of Old Testament teaching: Deuteronomy 6:4–5, Joshua 22:5 and 23:11.

Note that *love* as used in these verses is far different from our popular view of love. The love commanded here is a matter of devotion, a choice that denotes one's allegiance. It can and should spring from heartfelt emotion, but in the ancient Near East, *love* was also a political term, indicating truehearted loyalty to one's king.*

Jesus did not come to do away with the Old Testament commandments but to fulfill them. Therefore he upholds the command to love God, but notice how Jesus elaborated on this commandment (read Matt. 22:35–40).

*From *Zondervan Study Bible,* notes on Joshua 22:5 (Grand Rapids, MI: Zondervan, 1995), 317.

Jesus might easily have separated loving God from loving other people, but he chose not to do so. Surely he chose his words carefully in this situation since those questioning him were looking to trap him. He deliberately connected loving God with loving other people, which is what we are commanded to do throughout the New Testament.

The word Jesus chose to convey the idea of "love" is *not* the Greek verb *phileo*, which expresses friendly affection—a feeling our culture tends to think of as love—but *agapao*, "the commitment of devotion that is directed by the will and can be commanded as a duty." Therefore, the love Jesus commands us to have toward God and people is a matter of choice and an act of devotion.

Here we have two ideas that converge: We are commanded (1) to love God with a whole heart and (2) to love our neighbor as ourselves. Therefore, every act and attitude of love you choose toward your mate can be an act of love for God if you devote it to the Lord. When you choose to devote your demonstration of love for each other as an act of love to God—loving your mate "as unto the Lord"—your love does double duty! It blesses your mate and pleases God because you are obeying his law of love!

Practice

Many people think of their love for God and their spiritual acts of devotion as separate from how they treat others in the course of everyday life. This ought not to be so. Today's exercise will help you discover how intricately your love relationship with God is woven together with God's command in the Bible that we love each other.

⧗ One of you will need to read the following passages aloud. As one reads, the other should underline any phrase that speaks of *our love relationship with God or obedience to God* and circle every phrase that speaks of *our love for others*. As you do this together, you will see the interplay God designed between our loving him and loving others.

"Dear friends, let us love one another, for love comes from God. Everyone who loves has been born of God and knows God. Whoever does not love does not know God, because God is love. This is how God showed his love among us: He sent his one and only Son into the world that we might live through him. This is love: not that we loved God, but that he loved us and sent his Son as an atoning sacrifice for our sins. Dear friends, since God so loved us, we also ought to love one another. No one has ever seen God; but if we love one another, God lives in us and his love is made complete in us" (1 John 4:7–12).

"We love because he first loved us. If anyone says, 'I love God,' yet hates his brother, he is a liar. For anyone who does not love his brother, whom he has seen, cannot love God, whom he has not seen. And he has given us this command: Whoever loves God must also love his brother" (1 John 4:19–21).

These are just two of the passages where our love for others is connected to our love for and obedience to God. If you would like to explore this further you can look up the following: John 13:34–35; Romans 13:8–10; 1 Corinthians 13; 1 Peter 1:22–23; 1 John 3:11–19, 3:23–24; and 2 John 1:5–6.

⧖ In response to the verses you circled and underlined, answer the following questions.

1. Can you think of any circumstances where God excuses us from loving each other because we are "too busy" loving him?
   Husband (circle one): Yes / No　　　Wife (circle one): Yes / No

2. If you circled yes, list the circumstances and why you believe this to be true: _____

3. Can you think of times in your life when you were so busy working for God or demonstrating religious devotion that you neglected to love your mate? Husband (circle one): Yes / No　　　Wife (circle one): Yes / No

4. If you circled yes, perhaps you will want to identify these times and apologize.

⧖ This next self-quiz will help you gauge what activities you believe demonstrate love for God. Take the next *three minutes* and *quickly* jot down a list of what you currently do to demonstrate your love for God. (It's OK for you to have duplicate answers.)

Husband's List　　　　　　　　　　　　Wife's List

_____　　　　_____

_____　　　　_____

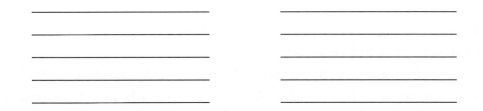

———————————————   ———————————————

———————————————   ———————————————

———————————————   ———————————————

———————————————   ———————————————

———————————————   ———————————————

⌛ When you each finish your list, answer the following questions.

1. How many of the items on your list had to do with acts of religious devotion such as tithing, praying at meals, giving thanks to God, going to church, worshiping, obeying God's commands, not doing anything illegal, giving service in church, witnessing, supporting missionaries, and so on? Husband: _____ Wife: _____

2. How many of the items on your list had to do with acts and attitudes of love you show each other (and those closest to you) in everyday life, such as giving your mate a back rub at the end of a long day, being patient enough to listen carefully, giving words of encouragement or a special gift to your mate, not being rude, and so on? Husband: _____ Wife: _____

If you find that your list has more of the former than the latter, you are not alone. Many Christians measure the "true test of a saint's life" in religious duties and rituals more than in acts and attitudes of love. In the Scriptures, the great miracle of the incarnation, the great revelation of God, slips into the ordinary parts of life. Consider the following quote by Oswald Chambers.

> The true test of a saint's life is not successfulness but faithfulness on the human level of life. We tend to set up success in Christian work as our purpose, but our purpose should be to display the glory of God in human life, to live a life "hidden with Christ in God" in our everyday human conditions (Colossians 3:3). Our human relationships are the very conditions in which the ideal life of God should be exhibited.*

*Oswald Chambers, *My Utmost for His Highest*, ed. James Reimann (Grand Rapids, MI: Discovery House, 1992), Nov. 16.

Share with each other how you previously judged your spiritual "success" and whether you gave yourself credit for spiritual success when you were being faithful on the human level of life.

Faith in God and love should go together since God is love. However, if you had to compare which is greater—faith or love—which would you choose? _____ (Hint: The answer can be found in 1 Cor. 13:13).

⧗ This practice exercise wouldn't be complete unless you actually put your love into action in your everyday lives. While you bear in mind that every act of love you show each other can be devoted to God, look for ways in the next twenty-four hours to demonstrate your love for God by loving each other. For example, situations may arise in which you might be impatient or quick to anger. Instead, with the help of the Holy Spirit, be patient and slow to anger. If memories of past hurts come up and bring to mind a list of wrongs you hold against your mate, choose not to keep account of those wrongs. Instead, choose to forgive as Christ forgave you. When you see a need in your mate's life that you might easily pretend not to notice, leap at the chance to help, showing him or her love—and in your heart devote that act of love as a demonstration of your love for God too.

Record 1 John 3:18 here in your own handwriting:
Wife: _____

_____

Husband: _____

_____

⧗ When you meet tomorrow, start your time together by thanking each other for the way you demonstrated love to each other. Share how it blessed you.

Promises

God's Promise to You
"And so we know and rely on the love God has for us. God is love. Whoever lives in love lives in God, and God in him" (1 John 4:16).

Your Promise to Each Other

To practice demonstrating your love for God by demonstrating love for each other.

Prayer

Our Father in heaven,

Oh how we long to love you as we should. Please forgive us for the times when we neglected loving each other while we were "too busy" doing religious things. Lord, please help us love you with all our heart, soul, mind, and strength, and to love each other as we love ourselves. Help us see every act of love we show each other as a gift of love to you. Amen!

Day Four
Be Equally Yoked Together
with Jesus as Your Master

Purpose

- To understand what it means when Jesus says "take my yoke upon you" and what it means to be "equally yoked together" with your mate

- To see how you can live as those who are equally yoked together in Jesus' yoke

- To commit to learn of Jesus as those who are yoked together in his yoke

Premise

Most Christians are familiar with the teaching that we are not to be "unequally yoked together" with unbelievers. The concept of being yoked together was familiar to the people living in Palestine in the first century. They lived in an agricultural society where they regularly saw oxen or other animals linked together in a yoke. The yoke united them to go the same direction and combine their strength to accomplish some task under a master.

When Paul told the early church not to be yoked together with unbelievers (in 2 Cor. 6:14–7:1), he was warning of the dangers of being united with those who serve false gods. No good purpose of God's kingdom can be served by putting yourself under the constraints of such a partnership. The Old Testament forbids yoking different kinds of animals (an ox and a donkey) together, so Paul's audience understood the concept of not being unequally yoked together.

As Christians, we are not just called *out* of partnership with unbelievers. We are also called *into* a better kind of partnership—with God and other believers. Today, you will consider what it means to be equally joined together under the yoke of Jesus Christ. Jesus said, "Come to me, all you who are weary and burdened, and I will give you rest. Take my yoke upon you and learn from me, for I am gentle and humble in heart, and you will find rest for your souls. For my yoke is easy and my burden is light" (Matt. 11:28–30).

Consider the various aspects of being equally yoked together under Jesus.

Equally Yoked

The opposite of being unequally yoked together is to be equally yoked, with another of the same kind. All who are in God's kingdom are sons and daughters of the Father.

Consider the following Scriptures and their implications for our being equals in God's kingdom. Summarize what each of the passages say about all believers being equals.

1 Corinthians 12:14–27 _____

_____

Romans 8:15–17 _____

_____

Galatians 3:26–4:7 _____

_____

Yoked

The idea of being under a yoke brought with it the remembrance of being in slavery. When the Jews were slaves in Egypt, they were treated like animals and forced to wear a yoke to carry heavy burdens. This made the yoke a symbol of shame.

Jesus' call to wear a yoke probably reminded the Jews of the promise found in Leviticus 26:9–13: "I will look on you with favor and make you fruitful and increase your numbers, and I will keep my covenant with you. You will still be eating last year's harvest when you will have to move it out to make room for the new. I will put my dwelling place among you, and I will not abhor you. I will walk among you and be your God, and you will be my people. I am the LORD your God, who brought you out of Egypt so that you would no longer be slaves to the Egyptians; I broke the bars of your yoke and enabled you to walk with heads held high."

Compare Matthew 11:28–30 and Leviticus 26:9–13. Discuss how Jesus' yoke is different from the yoke the slaves wore in Egypt.

Under the Same Master

Whoever owned the yoke was the master of those who were under it. To take Jesus' yoke upon you implies that Jesus is your master. When the two of you agree to live equally joined together under Jesus' yoke, you are acknowledging that Jesus is your master.

Going the Same Way

Whenever two are yoked together, they must go the same direction. When Jesus calls his followers to take his yoke upon them, he expects that they will follow him and go his way.

Read Matthew 7:13–14 and discuss these questions: What is characteristic of the way Jesus calls us to go? Does this imply there will be some decisions you will make together that run contrary to popular culture?

Practice

Think of one way the two of you do or can treat each other as equals in God's kingdom: _____

_____

_____

How do you already submit yourselves to Jesus as your master? _____

_____

_____

What have you both learned of Jesus—especially his gentle nature and humility?

_____

_____

⌛ What would you be willing to do to refresh your learning of Jesus himself? Circle any that apply or add your own ideas: Read the gospels again. Watch a biblically accurate video account of Jesus' life (for example, *The Visual Bible* or the Jesus film project). Meditate on Jesus' sermons. Other: _____

_____

What have the two of you felt led of the Lord to do that caused you to go a way contrary to popular opinion? _____

_____

⌛ Can you think of any situations or relationships where you are unequally yoked together with unbelievers? _____ If so, how can you help each other move out of those relationships and replace them with relationships where you're equally yoked?

Promises

God's Promise to You
"Take my yoke upon you and learn from me, for I am gentle and humble in heart, and *you will find rest for your souls.* For my yoke is easy and my burden is light" (Matt. 11:29–30).

Your Promise to Each Other
To be equally yoked together in Jesus' yoke.

Prayer

Our Father in heaven,

Thank you for having freed us from the slavery we have known in the past. Thank you for sending Jesus Christ to offer us his yoke, that we might serve you rather than ourselves or any other master. Thank you that his yoke is easy and his burden is light. Thank you that we are not unequally yoked in marriage with an unbeliever. Please help us make the most of being equally yoked with each other.

Please continue to reveal to us what it means when Jesus says to "take my yoke upon you and learn of me" and what it means to be "equally yoked together" with each other. May we stay on the narrow road, walk our Christian walk side by side, treat each other as equals, and bring glory to you by doing so. In the name of Jesus, our master. Amen!

Day Five
Review and Recommit Yourselves to Your Marriage Vows

Purpose

- To reconsider the importance of covenant relationships and vows before God

- To reconsider what your marriage vows really mean

- To reaffirm your marriage vows and your commitment to each other

Premise

Our culture has minimized the importance of marriage vows or any kind of sacred vow, but God has not. That is why we need to correct our lack of respect for our marriage vows by looking at the sacred view of the vows that are made to God regarding our marriage commitment.

Read the following verses that deal with making vows:

- *Moses on making vows:* Numbers 30:1–16 and Deuteronomy 23:21–23

- *Solomon on keeping vows:* Ecclesiastes 5:4–7 and Proverbs 2, especially verses 16–17

- *The prophet Malachi on keeping marriage vows:* Malachi 2:13–16

- *Jesus on the sanctity of marriage and keeping marriage vows:* Matthew 19:3–12

We see from all these passages of Scripture that marriage truly is *holy* matrimony. Marriage vows are made *to God* regarding our marriage partner, not just to each other.

If you have experienced adultery or divorce—the two most grievous ways that marriage vows can be broken—you may focus on what has happened in the past. If these have happened and you have not fully dealt with them, be sure to seek pastoral or other biblical counseling. However, for today, don't focus on the past. Instead trust that God forgives all sin—even adultery or divorce. Consider the more common and less blatant ways Christian couples need to attend to their marriage vows. Focus on aiming to become more faithful to the whole intent of your vows, now and in the future.

Practice

Start with a Positive Accounting
Below are a list of the common phrases used in Christian marriage vows. After each one, think of some ways you have kept this part of your vows. If you can't think of any, maybe your mate can remind you of times he or she can recall.
⌛ If time is short, list one in each category.
To love. . . . I have kept or keep this part of my vows when I . . .

Husband	Wife
_____	_____
_____	_____
_____	_____

To cherish. . . . I have nurtured, prized, treasured, treated you with honor by . . .

Husband	Wife
_____	_____
_____	_____
_____	_____

In sickness. . . . I minister to you when you are sick by . . .

Husband	Wife
_____	_____
_____	_____
_____	_____

And in health. . . . I bless you when we are both healthy by . . .

Husband   Wife

_____   _____

_____   _____

_____   _____

For richer. . . . I bless you in times when we are richer by . . .

Husband   Wife

_____   _____

_____   _____

_____   _____

And for poorer. . . . I stand by you and face life with you when we are poorer by . . .

Husband   Wife

_____   _____

_____   _____

_____   _____

To have and to hold. . . . I bless you in our exclusive physical relationship (this can include more than sex; a back rub or holding hands counts!) by . . .

Husband   Wife

_____   _____

_____   _____

_____   _____

Keeping myself only unto you. . . . I have kept myself only unto you (if there have been times when you have failed in this area, focus on how you have repented and what you are *currently* doing to keep yourself devoted exclusively to your mate), and I take care of myself to bless you by . . .

Husband   Wife

_____   _____

_____   _____

_____   _____

For better. . . . I bless you when things are going better by . . .

Husband   Wife

_____   _____

_____   _____

_____   _____

Or for worse. . . . I help you when things are going worse by . . .

Husband   Wife

_____   _____

_____   _____

_____   _____

Until death do we part. . . .

When you both finish writing the lists above, share with each other what it means to you to know that your mate is committed to a lifelong marriage with you.

⧖ *Take a Serious View of Where You Have Fallen Short of Keeping Your Vows*
While you want to take a positive view of your commitment to each other, don't minimize areas where you may not have kept your vows as God would have you.

If you see an area where you have fallen short, acknowledge where you have failed, ask your mate to forgive you, and recommit yourself to focus on keeping that part of your vows.

If there has been infidelity or some major breach, you may need the help of a counselor or pastor to help you navigate the troubled waters such a breach can create.

No matter how either of you have failed in keeping your marriage vows, God can forgive you, help you forgive each other, and make your marriage better than ever. God can help you start today with a fresh commitment to each other, and he can help you keep it.

Promises

God's Promise to You
"But if we walk in the light, as he is in the light, we have fellowship with one another, and the blood of Jesus, his Son, purifies us from all sin" (1 John 1:7–9).

Your Promise to Each Other
To recommit yourselves to keep your marriage vows, by God's grace.

Prayer

Our Father in heaven,

Thank you for giving us the sacred opportunity to be married to each other. Thank you for the blessings, as well as the challenges, that marriage brings. Thank you for allowing us to enter into sacred vows with each other and for joining our lives together as you promised.

As we considered each phrase of those vows, we saw where we have fallen short. In all these areas, convict our hearts. Help us confess, forgive us, and help us forgive each other. Please show us how to treat each other as we have promised—and give us the power to follow through. Please change our hearts and minds so that we may fulfill our renewed commitment to treat each other as you would have us.

Lord, please fill our marriage with so much love that you are glorified. Amen!

WEEK TWO

Unite to Worship, Praise,
and Give Thanks Together

Introduction

This week the two of you will experience intimacy with God and each other through worship, praise, and thanksgiving. This may feel somewhat awkward at first. However, as you venture beyond your comfort zone into new expressions of love for God and each other, you will surely be rewarded.

We will look at many different forms of worship modeled for us in the Bible. Some of these may be in keeping with your spiritual tradition or experience; others may be completely new to you. If you are distracted from God by any of the things that are outside your comfort zone, don't feel like you have to do them to be spiritual. God looks at your heart. Be as genuine as possible in your worship. As you both venture closer to God together, you can take greater risks spiritually and perhaps find joy and a deeper spiritual experience in ways as yet unfamiliar to you.

Your spiritual expression of worship and your comfort level with various forms of worship may differ from your mate's. This will be influenced by your personalities—whether you are more expressive or more reflective—by your previous worship experiences, and perhaps by how you're feeling on a particular day. Be careful to allow yourself and your mate room to express yourselves in worship that feels genuine, given where you each are in your personal relationship with God. It may help to close your eyes when you are worshiping God so that you don't get distracted by considering how your mate is expressing himself or herself.

Man to Man

with Bill McCartney

Someone once defined intimacy as "into-me-see." Jesus beckons us to come closer. We need to tell God that we love him every day. Isn't it interesting how God tells us every day in many ways that he loves us? He wants us to echo back our affections to him. That is what worship does in our relationship with God.

And is there any woman who does not wish to be told daily that she is loved? Our wives desire sincerity, sensitivity, and singularity as we focus on them. This brings to mind an old saying: "Do you love me? Do you love me not? You told me once but I forgot."

Worshiping God and giving thanks to him should run parallel to expressing love, affection, and gratitude for our wives. This week you get to practice doing both.

Woman to Woman

with Lyndi McCartney

This week you will experience the most intimate relationship the two of you can have with the Lord. This can make some people nervous. If so, don't hesitate to pray together that the Lord will open your hearts and abolish your inhibitions. You may be quite at home and comfortable in this chapter. Or you may find it awkward to worship God with each other at first. Deep intimacy can be a scary thing—even intimacy with God. If you have trouble with intimacy in other areas of life, you may instinctively hold back from being intimate with God alongside your husband.

I remember something Bill Hybels said at a Promise Keepers conference a few years ago. He said, "Some of you are not here by choice; a friend dragged you here. I saw the skid marks in the parking lot." If you are feeling like that at the thought of entering into worship with your husband, might I suggest that you take your shoes off. Worshiping God together is the closest we humans can come to standing on holy ground. With your husband, enter into this intimate time with the Lord and watch his glory fill your lives. This is a precious experience that will bless you as you enter into it together.

I'll confess that worshiping the Lord in song was hard for me. We sing songs to the Lord in the car all the time. But worshiping the Lord in song on command threw me for a loop. It's like sex. I just can't drop dead do it on cue. I need a warming, loving time. That's why I suggested prayer beforehand. It's OK if you pray a long time. That loving time with the Lord warms my heart and sets my inhibitions aside and then my heart can cry out in songs of love to him. Worshiping the Lord in song with my husband blesses me deeply. It gives me a spirit of patience and compassion for all my other encounters during the day. Praising the Lord and thanking the Lord were easy for me, but singing was hard. Who knew? Whatever may feel awkward for you, don't let that stop you. It takes time to grow comfortable worshiping the Lord together. Keep at it.

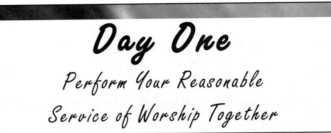

Day One
Perform Your Reasonable Service of Worship Together

Purpose

- To learn how to present your bodies as living sacrifices to God, which is your reasonable service of worship

- To present yourselves to God as living sacrifices

- To help each other continue to present yourselves to God as living sacrifices

Premise

One of the primary purposes of life is to worship God. Much of the history recorded for our instruction in Scripture has to do with worship. Sometimes it offers pictures of what it means to worship God as he desires. Sometimes it warns against worshiping anyone or anything other than God. We even see in the temptation of Jesus that Satan tried to get Jesus to bow down and worship him. Matthew 4:8–10 records, "Again, the devil took him to a very high mountain and showed him all the kingdoms of the world and their splendor. 'All this I will give you,' he said, 'if you will bow down and worship me.'

"Jesus said to him, 'Away from me, Satan! For it is written: "Worship the Lord your God, and serve him only."'"

Therefore, your first spiritual act is to enter into worship of God together. You may think of worship as singing songs side by side in a church service, but worship is so much more than that. Today you can begin to enter into the kind of worship God desires, together.

Paul's letter to the Romans focuses on one aspect of your spiritual service of worship. Open your Bible to Romans 12 and read verses 1 and 2. This passage brings out six points that form the basis for worshiping God:

1. You are to present your bodies to God as a living sacrifice.

2. You are holy and pleasing to God (this is by virtue of the righteousness of Jesus).

3. Your reasonable service of worship is to present your bodies to God as living sacrifices.

4. You are not to be conformed to this world.

5. You are to be transformed by the renewing of your mind.

6. Once you worship God in this way *then* you will be able to test and approve what God's good, pleasing, and perfect will is.

Practice

⧗ *Make a decision to present your body to God as a living sacrifice.* This is your reasonable service of worship. The Greek word translated "reasonable" is *logikos*, meaning logical or rational. Your worship of God is to be logical as a result of a rational choice to give your body to God as a living sacrifice. Will you?

Think about what this would mean. What would it mean for you to give your eyes to God (to not look at things that cause you to sin, to not look at anyone or anything covetously that is not yours, to look only at things that are pure)? What would it mean for you to give your brain to God (to use your intelligence in his service, to not use your knowledge or intelligence to do anything contrary to his will, to think of ways to please him and bless others)? What would it mean to give your mouth to God (to refrain from cursing, slander, and gossip; to speak only what gives grace to the hearer; to praise God and bless people by what you say, using your voice to worship God and share his good news with others)? What would it mean for you to give your hands to God (to serve him and others, to reach out to comfort others, to touch nothing that is unholy or illegal)? What would it mean to give your appetites—both sexual and physical—over to God? What would it mean to give your feet to God (to go only to those places God would have you go, to play sports in a way that honors God, to run to help others in need, to follow Jesus but not follow the ways of the world that lead to sin)?

What would it mean to give your ears to God (to refuse to listen to gossip, slander, or coarse jesting; to learn to listen to God's Word, God's voice; to hear only what is good, pure, excellent, and worthy of praise)? Will you choose to give your entire body to God as a living sacrifice? If so, take turns repeating the phrases of this prayer to God:

Dear Lord,

I present my body to you. I present my eyes to you. I present my brain to you. I present my mouth to you. I present my hands to you. I present my appetites to you. I present my feet to you. I present my ears to you. I present all that I am to you. Thank you for making me acceptable in your eyes! In Jesus' name. Amen!

⧖ *Agree with God that you are already holy and pleasing to him.* This is also a rational choice. God's Word says that you are a holy and acceptable sacrifice to God. You have been made holy on the basis of what Jesus Christ did for you on the cross. God calls you to accept this by faith. When you do, you will stop working to become acceptable to God and begin worshiping God because you have already been made holy by Jesus.

Look up the following verses to bolster your faith that you are holy and acceptable to God in Christ Jesus: 1 Peter 2:5; Ephesians 1:3–10; Colossians 1:22–23; 2 Timothy 1:9–10; Hebrews 2:11, 3:1, 10:9–14.

⧖ *Refuse to be conformed to the pattern of this world.* This world system exerts pressure on every Christian. The image the world would have us take on is very different from the image of Christ Jesus that God is transforming us into (as stated in Romans 8:29: "For those God foreknew he also predestined to be conformed to the likeness of his Son"). You know where the pressures come in your life that would make you be more worldly rather than more like Christ. Help each other come up with a few areas where you are currently feeling the most pressure to conform to this world rather than to the image of Christ.

Husband's Pressures   Wife's Pressures

_____   _____

_____   _____

_____   _____

Share these pressures with each other and talk about your resolution to resist them. Agree to encourage each other in these areas.

⧗ *Resist being pressured into the world's mold—by the renewing of your mind.* The remedy to being pressured into the world's pattern is to be *transformed by the renewing of your mind.* Being transformed is a process. You can devote your whole body to God today, but it will take time to be transformed by the renewing of your mind. Choose one area that gives you trouble currently. It may be your eyes— looking at pornography. It may be your tongue—speaking sharply, harshly, or with words inclined to slander and gossip. It may be your mind—thinking judg-mentally or thinking of yourself as better than other people. Choose one area and *decide* to begin filling your mind with what God says about that part of your body and how you should use it.

⧗ *Tell each other what you plan to do to renew your mind with regard to the area in your life that has yielded too much to the world's pressures.* Then do it a little each day. And when you notice any positive changes in your mate's chosen area, don't spare the compliments!

Promises

God's Promise to You
"Do not conform any longer to the pattern of this world, but be transformed by the renewing of your mind. Then you will be able to test and approve what God's will is—his good, pleasing and perfect will" (Rom. 12:2).

Your Promise to Each Other
To compliment each other on positive changes.

Prayer

Our Father in heaven,

Thank you for making us holy and pleasing in your sight by the blood of Jesus. Thank you that when we bring our bodies to you, you deem us acceptable sacrifices.

Lord, when we think of giving our bodies to you, we can think of many ways we misuse our bodies. Please convict our hearts, forgive us, and change us. You said this is our reasonable service of worship. We've thought it over and we choose to devote our bodies to you so that we may be transformed by you. In Jesus' name we pray. Amen!

Day Two
Worship God Together with the Right Attitude

Purpose

- To understand the right attitude we are to have when we worship God

- To worship God together with the right attitude

- To bow down and kneel humbly before God as we worship

Premise

The Old Testament term for worship meant to prostrate oneself, to bow down in homage to royalty or God. The New Testament term used for worship came from the word that meant to kiss (like a dog licking his master's hand), to prostrate oneself in homage, to do reverence, to adore. Worship is as much a position before God and an attitude of heart as it is something we do on Sunday morning.

Worship is far more than saying or singing the right words. The prophet Isaiah (and Jesus who later quoted the prophet) condemned those who said the right words or sang the right songs but had the wrong attitude of heart. Jesus told the Pharisees and teachers of the law, "You hypocrites! Isaiah was right when he prophesied about you: 'These people honor me with their lips, but their hearts are far from me. They worship me in vain; their teachings are but rules taught by men'" (Matt. 15:7–9).

These men were professional religious leaders, yet their wrong attitude nullified their acts of worship. In contrast, Jesus went out of his way to meet with a woman who had broken all the rules. She was a Samaritan (who had intermarried with a non-Jew in violation of Old Testament law) who worshiped God in the wrong place, had married and divorced five times, and lived with a man who was not her husband. Yet Jesus went to her to tell her what kind of people God the Father sought to worship him.

Jesus had struck up a conversation with her at Jacob's well in Samaria. When it became apparent to her that Jesus was a prophet, she asked him about the proper way to worship. She said, "Our fathers worshiped on this mountain, but you Jews claim that the place where we must worship is in Jerusalem."

Jesus declared, "Believe me, woman, a time is coming when you will worship the Father neither on this mountain nor in Jerusalem. You Samaritans worship what you do not know; we worship what we do know, for salvation is from the Jews. Yet a time is coming and has now come when the true worshipers will worship the Father in spirit and truth, for they are the kind of worshipers the Father seeks. God is spirit, and his worshipers must worship in spirit and in truth."

The woman said, "I know that Messiah" (called Christ) "is coming. When he comes, he will explain everything to us."

Then Jesus declared, "I who speak to you am he" (John 4:20–26).

Jesus describes true worshipers as those who worship the Father in _____ and in _____.

What do you think this means for you? (Share this aloud with your partner.)

How do you prepare your heart and spirit to worship God that is different from how the Pharisees worshiped God? (Share this aloud with your partner.)

What do you think it means to worship God in truth? (Share this aloud with your partner.)

Are you willing to worship God in spirit and in truth? _____

Read the verses that follow, and note the attitude of heart that is addressed in each.

> Come, let us bow down in worship, let us kneel before the LORD our Maker; for he is our God and we are the people of his pasture, the flock under his care. (Ps. 95:6–7).

Are you willing to bow down and kneel humbly before God as you worship him? _____

Shout for joy to the LORD, all the earth. Worship the LORD with gladness; come before him with joyful songs. (Ps. 100:1–2)

Are you willing to rejoice and sing with gladness as you worship God? _____

Therefore, since we are receiving a kingdom that cannot be shaken, let us be thankful, and so worship God acceptably with reverence and awe, for our "God is a consuming fire." (Heb. 12:28–29)

Are you willing to approach God with reverence and awe? _____

Practice

Your practice today will be to worship God together with a right attitude. As you worship God in the privacy of your home, spend some of your time on your knees, bowing down humbly before God, some in joyful shouting, and some in reverential awe.

⧗ Choose from the following to help you enter into worship together.

- Choose a recording of worship songs you both know.

- Find a hymnal that has songs you both know. Choose a few songs that allow you to worship God, rather than those that tell a story or proclaim some truth. (For example, "How Great Thou Art" worships God, while "Amazing Grace" tells a story of what God has done.)

- Recall praise and worship songs you both know by heart.

⧗ Do the following together.

1. Make a list of several songs that will keep you singing for at least fifteen minutes, or agree to sing a selection of worship songs from a tape.

2. Eliminate all possible interruptions (unplug the telephone and so on).

3. Bow down on your knees and set your hearts toward the Lord with the right attitude.

4. Sing one song after another, keeping your hearts and minds set on the Lord as you worship him together. Don't stop to talk between songs.

Promises

God's Promise to You
"The true worshipers will worship the Father in spirit and truth, for they are the kind of worshipers *the Father seeks*" (John 4:23).

Your Promise to Each Other
To do nothing that will distract your mate from worshiping God during times set apart for worship.

Prayer

Our Father in heaven,

We worship you! What a privilege it is to worship you! Thank you Father for seeking us to worship you. Lord we humble ourselves before you. We do not fully comprehend how awesome you are, yet we long to worship you as you deserve to be worshiped. Thank you for welcoming not just those who are religious professionals but any who will come to you in spirit and truth. Lord, we want our hearts to be near you when we worship. Please help us set our hearts and minds in the right direction when we come before you. Please let our hearts be near you whenever our lips are employed in worshiping you. Please help us to worship you together more often. Amen!

Day Three

Praise God Together

Purpose

- To understand what it means to praise God as he desires

- To praise God together

- To share your praise of God with each other on an ongoing basis

Premise

The Bible is full of admonitions telling us to "Praise the Lord!" The Old Testament uses various words with similar meanings translated as "praise." Some of these mean to boast, celebrate, sing a hymn, laud, revere or worship with extended hands, shout or address in a loud voice, make a joyful noise! The New Testament also uses various words that tell us how to praise God. These also have a variety of meanings including to tell a story that brings praise to God, worship, applaud, commend, give glory, honor, celebrate God in song. All these definitions carry a sense of intensity as we show our praise. None of them is passive.

Hebrews 13:15 tells us, "Through Jesus, therefore, let us continually offer to God a sacrifice of praise—the fruit of lips that confess his name." Those who drew near to God in worship under the Old Covenant were told to bring many kinds of sacrifices. Under the New Covenant we no longer have to bring animal sacrifices, or fruits, or grains. However, we are told to bring a sacrifice of praise, the fruit of our lips. This is not to be done just in church, but continually. Since you live together, you can encourage each other to praise God continually, every chance you get in the course of daily life.

Praise not only pleases God but it also exerts power in the spiritual realm. Psalm 22:3 tells us that God inhabits or is enthroned in the praises of his people. Second Chronicles 5:12–14 tells us that corporate praise preceded God's glory filling Solomon's temple. Second Chronicles 20:12–26 tells what happened when King Jehoshaphat used praise to confront armies that were more powerful than his army. This story shows that praise is a powerful unseen force in God's kingdom. Consider what happened.

> After consulting the people, Jehoshaphat appointed men to sing to the LORD and to praise him for the splendor of his holiness as they went out at the head of the army, saying: "Give thanks to the LORD, for his love endures forever." As they began to sing and praise, the LORD set ambushes against the men of Ammon and Moab and Mount Seir who were invading Judah, and they were defeated. The men of Ammon and Moab rose up against the men from Mount Seir to destroy and annihilate them. After they finished slaughtering the men from Seir, they helped to destroy one another.
>
> When the men of Judah came to the place that overlooks the desert and looked toward the vast army, they saw only dead bodies lying on the ground; no one had escaped. So Jehoshaphat and his men went to carry off their plunder, and they found among them a great amount of equipment and clothing and also articles of value—more than they could take away. There was so much plunder that it took three days to collect it. On the fourth day they assembled in the Valley of Beracah, where they praised the LORD. This is why it is called the Valley of Beracah (which means praise) to this day. (2 Chron. 20:21–26)

Here are several ways you can praise God continually in your daily lives.

- Boast to each other about the great things God has done for you.

- Daily praise God to each other for his love, his kindness, his goodness, and so on.

- Praise the Lord by reminding each other of his benefits (see Ps. 103).

- Go about the house celebrating God with songs.

- Fill your house and car with praise music on radio, tape, or CD.

- If either of you play a musical instrument, use it to praise the Lord (see Ps. 150).

- Join a choir together and praise God with a large group (see Ps. 68:26).

- Sing songs in praise of God with outstretched arms.

- Clap your hands and shout to God in joyful praise (see Ps. 47:1).

Practice

⧗ Take turns boasting to each other about how great God is and what you have seen him do that is praiseworthy. If time is short, boast of God's greatness in just one thing.

Make a list of several songs you both know that praise God. Be sure to choose some that you can sing together. Choose some that praise God for his nature and his goodness and his love that endures forever.

Sing as many of these songs together as you have time for. Sing with gusto! Don't let the quality of your voices discourage you; encourage each other for the sincerity of your hearts. God said to make a joyful *noise.*

⧗ As time allows, try one or more of the following worship options if they feel comfortable.

While you are singing, do some of the things implied by the various definitions of praise given in God's Word: extend your hands to the Lord, leap for joy, clap, make a joyful noise with a musical instrument.

Open your Bible to one of the praise psalms such as Psalm 47, 92, 103–7, or 150. Take turns reading praise verses aloud, saying each verse to the Lord with a strong voice as one who is boasting in the Lord.

If you are dealing with a spiritual battle where the forces arrayed against you seem too much for you, do what King Jehoshaphat did: Precede any spiritual battle with planned sessions of praise. Agree to praise God in faith before dealing with these enemies of your soul. You may be as amazed as they were to see the Lord go before you and set ambushes for your enemies.

Promises

God's Promise to You
"But you are a chosen people, a royal priesthood, a holy nation, a people belonging to God, that you may declare the praises of him who called you out of darkness into his wonderful light" (1 Pet. 2:9).

Your Promise to Each Other
To encourage each other as you praise God in everyday life.

Prayer

Our Father in heaven,

We praise you! We praise you for your goodness! We praise you for your love that endures forever! We praise you for all your benefits to us! We confess that we do not praise you nearly as much or as well as you deserve.

Lord, we want to continually bring a sacrifice of praise, the fruit of our lips, to you, that you may be glorified through us. Please help us to go about our daily lives with praise on our lips. Remind us to go forth with praise whenever we have a spiritual battle to fight. Help us to fill our home with praise to you. Please help us become more comfortable praising you with gusto. Help us change our hearts so that our enthusiasm for praising you is more than our enthusiasm for praising our favorite sports team or media star. Praise you, Lord! Together, we praise you, Lord! Amen.

Day Four

Give Thanks to God Together

Purpose

- To understand what Scripture teaches about giving thanks to God

- To give thanks to God together

- To encourage each other to give thanks in all circumstances

Premise

When we neglect to give thanks, God notices. In Luke 17:11–19, we read of Jesus healing ten men near the border between Samaria and Israel who had leprosy. "One of them, when he saw he was healed, came back, praising God in a loud voice. He threw himself at Jesus' feet and thanked him—and he was a Samaritan.

"Jesus asked, 'Were not all ten cleansed? Where are the other nine? Was no one found to return and give praise to God except this foreigner?' Then he said to him, 'Rise and go; your faith has made you well.'" Jesus expected that those he had benefited would come to him and give him thanks. That was the least they could do, but most of them neglected giving him the thanks he deserved.

God calls us to give thanks to him—which is only right. But often we take his blessings and benefits for granted. Giving thanks should be a commitment as well as the overflow of a grateful heart. Nehemiah actually assigned two choirs to give thanks (Neh. 12:31). The psalms are full of admonitions to give thanks to God. We are told in 1 Chronicles 16:8, "Give thanks to the LORD, call on his name; make known among the nations what he has done." Over and over again the Scripture repeats, "Give thanks to the LORD, for he is good; his love endures forever." Psalm 100:4 tells us, "Enter his gates with thanksgiving and his courts with praise; give thanks to him and praise his name."

We see in the New Testament that Jesus remembered to give thanks to the Father—even though he is the Son of God.* He gave thanks at meals for what God provided. We too should remember to thank God for every meal he provides. First Corinthians 10:16 also reminds us to give thanks whenever we take communion and thereby participate in the blood and body of Christ.

The most familiar verse about giving thanks may also be the most confounding. First Thessalonians 5:18 says, "Give thanks in all circumstances, for this is God's will for you in Christ Jesus." We are to give thanks no matter what our circumstances, even when our circumstances are difficult. Note that the verse does not tell us to give thanks *for* all circumstances, but rather to give thanks *in* all circumstances. Even when our circumstances change for the worse, God does not change. There is still plenty for which we can be thankful. When we give thanks, it shows that we truly believe that God is good and his steadfast love endures forever.

Practice

⧗ Some of the things you will practice today may already be a part of your daily life. A basic custom of giving thanks is to thank God for every meal and every special blessing he provides (like a bonus, a promotion, or anything good that comes into your lives). If this has not been a part of your everyday life, make a commitment to each other to begin thanking God for every meal.

⧗ When setting an intentional time to practice giving thanks to God, it may help you to have a form to follow. God has given us such a form in Psalm 107. As you read it, you will see that it lays out many things for which people can give thanks to God. You can use the text of this psalm to create categories of the kinds of things to be thankful to God for.

List anything you can think of that happened in your life that falls into each category. For example, Psalm 107:2 says, "Let the redeemed of the LORD say this—those he redeemed from the hand of the foe." The category for thanksgiving would be for when God has redeemed you from a foe. You might say, "Lord, I thank you for the time I was being slandered by _____ and you redeemed my good name."

*See Matthew 14:19, 26:26–27; Mark 6:41, 8:7, 14:22–23; Luke 9:16, 22:17–19, 24:30; John 6:11, 11:41.

What Do You Have to Be Thankful For?

⧗ If time is short, pick out one or a few of the categories that are most relevant to your life at this time and share them with each other.

We have stated the categories in the form of questions, with the verse reference. If you think of something for which you can give thanks in that category, take turns giving thanks out loud before you go to the next item.

When has the Lord been good to you? (Ps. 107:1) *Lord, I'm thankful for your goodness when . . .*

When has the Lord redeemed you from a foe? (Ps. 107:2) *Lord, thank you for redeeming me from my foe when . . .*

When has the Lord delivered you from your distress when you cried out in trouble? (Ps. 107:6) *Lord, thank you for when I was in trouble and you . . .*

When has God showed you his unfailing love? (Ps. 107:8) *Lord, thank you for showing your love when . . .*

When has God done a wonderful deed for you? (Ps. 107:8) *Lord, thank you for the wonderful deeds you have shown me when . . .*

When has God satisfied your thirst or hunger with good things? (Ps. 107:9) *Lord, thank you for satisfying me when . . .*

When has God heard your cries and saved you from your distress even though you suffered because of your own rebellion against the Lord? (Ps. 107:10–13) *Lord, thank you for answering my cries when . . .*

When has God brought you out of darkness and the deepest gloom and broken your chains? (Ps. 107:14) *Lord, thank you for delivering me from darkness when . . . And thank you for breaking the chains of _____ that had me bound.*

When has the Lord sent his Word and healed you? (Ps. 107:20) *Lord, thank you for healing me when . . .*

When has the Lord calmed the storms in your life? (Ps. 107:23–30) *Lord, thank you for calming my storms and guiding me to a haven when . . .*

When has God blessed your labor and given you a fruitful harvest? (Ps. 107:33–38) *Lord, thank you for your blessing on my work when . . .*

When has God lifted you out of your affliction? (Ps. 107:41) *Lord, thank you for lifting me out of my affliction when I felt so needy because . . .*

Psalm 107 ends with this: "Whoever is wise, let him heed these things and consider the great love of the LORD." The more you give attention to all that the

Lord has done for you because of his great love, the more giving thanks will become part of your daily life.

Promises

God's Promise to You
"Forget not all his benefits—who forgives all your sins and heals all your diseases, who redeems your life from the pit and crowns you with love and compassion, who satisfies your desires with good things so that your youth is renewed like the eagle's" (Ps. 103:2–6).

Your Promise to Each Other
To encourage each other to give thanks to God at every meal and in all circumstances.

Prayer

Our Father in heaven,

You deserve our thanks far more than we have given it. Please forgive us for all that you have done for us that we have taken for granted. Please make us more aware of your blessings so that we might give you the thanks you deserve.

Lord, when we are in good circumstances, please help us not to forget that every good gift comes from you. When we are in difficult circumstances, help us remember to thank you, for your love for us endures in all circumstances.

Lord, we thank you today that we are together. We thank you that we are able to come together and share this time of thanksgiving. We thank you for all our blessings, for all that you provide, for all your promises, for all you have done for us in the past and will do for us in the future. We thank you for the way you have changed our lives and made us more like you. We thank you for your healing, your love, and your faithfulness to all generations. May we encourage each other to give you the thanks you deserve every day. Amen!

Day Five
Bless Each Other with Praise, Gratitude, and Thanks

Purpose

- To bless each other by speaking to each other in psalms, hymns, and spiritual songs

- To give thanks to each other whenever thanks are due

- To give each other praise when praise is due

- To express our gratitude to each other and to God for each other

Premise

When we look at Ephesians 5:17–20 and Colossians 3:15–17, we see that speaking God's Word *to one another* in psalms, hymns, and spiritual songs is associated with giving thanks to God the Father and having gratitude in our hearts. We are told in Psalm 100:4, "Enter his gates with thanksgiving and his courts with praise." Praise and thanksgiving pave the way into the presence of God. It is also interesting to note that the two passages that tell us to speak to each other within the context of praise and thanksgiving lead directly into sections of Scripture that deal with how husbands and wives should love each other and treat each other.

Could it be that speaking to each other with praise, gratitude, and thanksgiving may not only pave the way into God's presence but also pave the way into the kind of relationship where we treat each other as God would have us?

Read each of the following passages, noting the emphasis on speaking praise and thanksgiving to each other. Then open your Bible and read these passages in context; note how the following verses address how we are to relate to each other and love each other.

"Therefore do not be foolish, but understand what the Lord's will is. Do not get drunk on wine, which leads to debauchery. Instead, be filled with the Spirit. Speak to one another with psalms, hymns and spiritual songs. Sing and make music in your heart to the Lord, always giving thanks to God the Father for everything, in the name of our Lord Jesus Christ" (Eph. 5:17–20).

"Let the peace of Christ rule in your hearts, since as members of one body you were called to peace. And be thankful. Let the word of Christ dwell in you richly as you teach and admonish one another with all wisdom, and as you sing psalms, hymns and spiritual songs with gratitude in your hearts to God. And whatever you do, whether in word or deed, do it all in the name of the Lord Jesus, giving thanks to God the Father through him" (Col. 3:15–17).

Today, you will practice speaking God's Word—especially hymns recorded in Scripture—to each other. Then you will bless each other by expressing your gratitude and thanks and praising each other. Praising your mate is biblical. Much of the Song of Songs consists of Solomon and his bride praising each other.

Practice

Begin by obeying God's admonition to "Speak to one another with psalms, hymns and spiritual songs." Psalm 136 was written to be recited back and forth while giving thanks to God. One of you take the first part (on the left) and the other take the refrain, "His love endures forever." Read the entire psalm back and forth to each other.

Ps. 136:1—Give thanks to the LORD, for he is good.

> His love endures forever.

Ps. 136:2—Give thanks to the God of gods.

> His love endures forever.

Ps. 136:3—Give thanks to the Lord of lords:

> His love endures forever.

Ps. 136:4—to him who alone does great wonders,

> His love endures forever.

Ps. 136:5—who by his understanding made the heavens,

> His love endures forever.

Ps. 136:6—who spread out the earth upon the waters,

> His love endures forever.

Ps. 136:7—who made the great lights—

> His love endures forever.

Ps. 136:8—the sun to govern the day,

> His love endures forever.

Ps. 136:9—the moon and stars to govern the night;

> His love endures forever.

Ps. 136:10—to him who struck down the firstborn of Egypt

> His love endures forever.

Ps. 136:11—and brought Israel out from among them

> His love endures forever.

Ps. 136:12—with a mighty hand and outstretched arm;

> His love endures forever.

Ps. 136:13—to him who divided the Red Sea asunder

> His love endures forever.

Ps. 136:14—and brought Israel through the midst of it,

> His love endures forever.

Ps. 136:15—but swept Pharaoh and his army into the Red Sea;

> His love endures forever.

Ps. 136:16–to him who led his people through the desert,

> His love endures forever.

Ps. 136:17—who struck down great kings,

> His love endures forever.

Ps. 136:18—and killed mighty kings—

> His love endures forever.

Ps. 136:19—Sihon king of the Amorites

> His love endures forever.

Ps. 136:20—and Og king of Bashan—

> His love endures forever.

Ps. 136:21—and gave their land as an inheritance,

> His love endures forever.

Ps. 136:22—an inheritance to his servant Israel;

> His love endures forever.

Ps. 136:23—to the One who remembered us in our low estate

His love endures forever.

Ps. 136:24—and freed us from our enemies,

His love endures forever.

Ps. 136:25—and who gives food to every creature.

His love endures forever.

Ps. 136:26—Give thanks to the God of heaven.

His love endures forever.

This psalm recounts the victories God won on behalf of his people Israel. Together, come up with a written list of at least ten things God has done in your life that demonstrate that his love endures in your lives. Switch roles; have the one who read the psalm's refrain read each item on your list. After each item, have the second partner respond with, "His love endures forever."

⧗ Next you will express your gratitude, praise, and thanks to your partner.

- Make a list of three qualities you are grateful for in your mate.

- Make a list of three things for which you want to praise your mate (these could be personal attributes, accomplishments, something you especially like about him or her).

- Make a list of three things you want to thank your mate for doing for you or your family.

⧗ Once you have both completed your lists, take turns sharing your gratitude, praise, and thanks with each other.

Discuss how this could help pave the way for treating each other as God says we should. Are you more inclined to treat your mate well after hearing him or her praise and thank you? Hmmm . . . Does this give you any ideas?

Promises

God's Promise to You
"Do not judge, and you will not be judged. Do not condemn, and you will not be

condemned. Forgive, and you will be forgiven. Give, and it will be given to you. A good measure, pressed down, shaken together and running over, will be poured into your lap. For with the measure you use, it will be measured to you" (Luke 6:37–38).

Your Promise to Each Other

To express gratitude, praise, and thanks to each other as a regular part of your relationship.

Prayer

Our Father in heaven,

It seems somewhat strange for us to be speaking to each other in a psalm, yet there is such power in your Word. When we take the time to think of all that you have done to show your love for us, we can think of a lot more than we normally do. We often take you for granted although we don't mean to. The same is true of how we treat each other. When we take time to think of how much we have to be grateful for, to praise and to give thanks for in each other, we discover a lot.

Lord, please help us to make speaking to each other in psalms, hymns, and spiritual songs a regular part of our shared life. Also help us to make a point of expressing our gratitude, praise, and thanks to each other on a regular basis. In Jesus' name. Amen!

WEEK THREE

Pray Together

Introduction

This week we will focus on praying together. Praying together daily will have a tremendous influence, not only on your spiritual lives, but also on your marriage. Consider the following quote from *The Making of a Godly Man* by John Trent, "Statistics reveal that the divorce rate in the United States is roughly one in two—that is, one marriage out of every two will end in divorce. Tragically, the Gallup poll shows that the divorce rate for people who say they are evangelical Christians is no different from that of the general population. *But note one powerful difference that surfaced in the Gallup organization's extensive research of believers:* For those couples who pray together every night, the divorce rate goes from one in two to—hold on to your hat—*1 in 1,052.* (See Commissioned Research on 'Evangelical Christians,' Gallup Research Corporation summary report, May 1991.)"*

Keeping your marriage together is only one of the benefits of praying together as a couple. Each day we will consider and practice various ways you can pray with each other and for each other. On day one you will learn to share your cares with each other and turn your mate's cares into prayers that you will lift up to the Lord. On day two you will learn the power of agreeing together in prayer. On day three you will practice blessing each other by laying hands on each other in a prayer of blessing. On day four you will explore the area of prayer and fasting (of various kinds—not just

* John Trent, *The Making of a Godly Man Workbook* (Colorado Springs, CO: Focus on the Family Publishing, 1997).

fasting from food or drink) to address challenging spiritual strongholds and advance God's kingdom using this serious spiritual discipline. On day five you will practice turning God's Word into prayers that are sure to be in the will of God.

Nothing takes the place of prayer in the life of the believer. Certainly you will have times when you retreat to be alone to pray, as Jesus often did. But you will find both your marriage and spiritual lives strengthened considerably when you practice praying regularly with each other and for each other.

Man to Man
with Bill McCartney

In my opinion, God is looking for people who will carve out a special time each day to be with him just because they love him. Prayer is communion with God. When we pray with our mate, it becomes communion with God and each other. Is your life complicated? Want to simplify it? Prayer does that. God answers prayer. Kneeling, lying prostrate, reaching, longing, hungering after God puts everything in perspective. We rediscover who we are before a holy and righteous God. Is there anything richer, more rewarding, sustaining, and penetrating than praying blessings over one another? This pleases God and restores us. Who would dare let a day go by without using this privilege?

Woman to Woman
with Lyndi McCartney

This week is my favorite! I love to pray with and for my husband. And I absolutely treasure his prayers for me to the Lord. A few years ago I came across a verse in Malachi in the Living Bible translation that revolutionized the way I see my husband and the significance of prayer in our marriage. Malachi 2:15 reads, "You were united to your wife by the Lord. In God's wise plan, when you married, the two of you became one person in His sight." Of course, we've all heard many times that when you marry the two of you become one, but when my eyes saw, "one person in His sight," that made a huge difference to me. If God looks upon us as one, then my intercessory prayers for my husband and his for me are vital. Amos 3:3 says, "Do two walk together except they be agreed?" We didn't walk together very well, but we could stumble with the best of them. Praying for each other has significantly changed our lives, and when we pray together for anything that glorifies God, he answers *in the affirmative.*

Purpose

- To understand how God wants you to handle your cares, worries, and anxieties

- To listen to each other's cares well enough to turn them into prayers

- To lift each other's cares to God in an acceptable way that will bring God's peace

Premise

Your overall goal as you go through this workbook is to be sold out to God together—to seek first the kingdom of God and his righteousness. You can help each other become sold out completely to God by helping each other process a part of life that interferes with seeking God's kingdom—the tendency to worry and be anxious over the cares of this life. Open your Bible and read what Jesus taught in Matthew 6:25–34 then answer the following questions.

What specific aspects of life does Jesus tell us not to worry about? _____
_____
_____

What reasons does Jesus give to assure us that we need not worry about these things? _____
_____
_____

What does Jesus tell us to do rather than worry about these things? _____

_____

_____

What promise does Jesus make to us if we do what he says? _____

_____

_____

One way we can seek first the kingdom of God is to take all our cares to God in prayer. The Old Testament says it this way, "Cast your cares on the LORD and he will sustain you; he will never let the righteous fall" (Ps. 55:22). Peter urges all Christians, "Cast all your anxiety on him because he cares for you" (1 Pet. 5:7).

The practice of sharing your cares with each other and lifting your mate's cares up to the Lord has many benefits. By doing so, you remind each other and encourage each other to deal with the cares of this life in light of your faith in a loving God. Making a regular practice of taking your mate's cares before your Father in heaven will require the kind of sharing and listening that many married couples long for. Those who grow frustrated hearing their mate's problems because there is no way they can fix the problems can turn to prayer as something tangible they can do until the Lord shows them if there is some action they can take. Beyond all the relational benefits, God answers prayer! God can do far more than we dare to ask or even imagine. When the two of you begin to regularly lift up each other's cares in prayer, you will see not only benefits in your communication but also powerful answers wrought by the hand of God.

People tend to share their cares and anxieties with their marriage partner in one way or another. Often it comes in the form of griping, complaining, or arguing. This is not what God wants for his people. Philippians 2:14–15 says, "Do everything without complaining or arguing, so that you may become blameless and pure, children of God without fault in a crooked and depraved generation, in which you shine like stars in the universe." What you will learn today gives you a positive alternative to use whenever you find yourself or your mate complaining.

Practice

God's Instructions for Handling Anxieties

Do not be anxious about anything, but in everything, by prayer and petition, with thanksgiving, present your requests to God. (Phil. 4:6)

⧗ Your goal in this exercise is to interview you partner to find out what cares your mate is carrying and what is causing him or her to be anxious. As you listen, do your best to empathize with your partner's feelings, not to minimize them but rather to understand what is weighing on his or her heart. Also listen carefully enough so that you can take the particulars of the cares and anxieties and turn them into specific requests that you will then make to God on your mate's behalf.

⧗ After you have listened to the worries, cares, and anxieties, recite them back to make sure you understand what your spouse has tried to communicate.

⧗ List your partner's worries, cares, and anxieties here (limit yourself to about three items today; you have the rest of your lives together to process any more than that).

1. _____

2. _____

3. _____

Turn each of the cares, worries, or anxieties into a specific request that you will present to God the Father in the name of Jesus on your mate's behalf. For example, if your husband shares that he is worried because debts are piling up and he feels powerless to turn the financial situation around, turn that into a request like this: Father God, please help us get out of debt. Please show us how to better manage the finances we have or provide more money so that we can progress toward getting out of debt.

Requests

1. _____

_____

_____

2. _____

_____

_____

3. _____

_____

_____

After one of you has completed this, reverse roles and do the same for the other.

Listen to your partner's worries, cares, and anxieties, then recite them back to make sure you understand them. List your mate's worries, cares, and anxieties below.

1. _____

2. _____

3. _____

Turn each of the cares, worries, or anxieties into a specific request that you will present to God the Father in the name of Jesus on your mate's behalf.

Requests

1. _____

_____

_____

2. _____

_____

_____

3. _____

_____

_____

⧗ Once your lists of requests on each other's behalf are written, take turns praying the requests to the Father. After you have presented these cares to God, be sure to thank him. Thank him for caring for you, for promising to give you his peace when you bring your anxieties to him in this way, and for promising to move on your behalf. God may not answer each petition the way you want it answered. God knows better than we do what we truly need. However, you can be assured that God will move on your behalf with regard to your requests.

One of the things you can expect God to do when you turn your anxieties into requests in this way is to send his peace to guard your hearts and minds. Imagine that he is sending a security guard or sentry of peace to march around the perimeters of your minds and emotions to ward off any anxieties or worries that threaten you.

Promises

God's Promise to You
"Do not be anxious about anything, but in everything, by prayer and petition, with thanksgiving, present your requests to God. *And the peace of God, which transcends all understanding, will guard your hearts and your minds in Christ Jesus*" (Phil. 4:6–7).

Your Promise to Each Other
To remind each other and encourage each other to turn complaints, cares, worries, and anxieties into requests you present to God. And to offer to pray on each other's behalf when you notice your partner being anxious for anything.

Prayer

Our Father in heaven,

Thank you for caring for us enough to invite us to cast our anxieties on you. Thank you that we can know your peace that passes all understanding if we will turn our cares into requests. Thank you for hearing and answering our prayers in the ways that are best for us.

Lord, please help us be compassionate and tender-hearted toward each other. Help us be patient and caring enough to listen to those things that cause each of us to be worried and anxious. Lord, also help us to remind each other of your instructions that we are not to be anxious for anything, but to present everything before you in prayer with thanksgiving. Lord, help us encourage each other to obey these instructions so that we can know your peace in our lives. Amen!

Day Two

Agree Together in Prayer

Purpose

- To understand the power and importance of agreeing together in prayer

- To find areas where you already agree or can agree

- To agree together in prayer about specific things

Premise

Being a Christian couple gives you a tremendous advantage in your prayer life. Jesus taught that there is a special privilege of communion with God that comes when two people agree together in prayer. Since you live together, you have the continual opportunity to avail yourself of this privilege.

Jesus said, "Again, I tell you that if two of you on earth agree about anything you ask for, it will be done for you by my Father in heaven. For where two or three come together in my name, there am I with them" (Matt. 18:19–20). The word translated as agree here is the Greek word *sumphoneo*. It means to be in harmony with each other, to concur, to be of one accord. These terms relate to a musical analogy. If we get in tune with each other, we will experience God's presence and power in prayer. If we live in discord, out of tune with each other, each doing "our own thing," our prayers will not be as effective as they could be.

Many Christians struggle, having disagreements and dissension with other Christians. Paul wrote to the Corinthians, "I appeal to you, brothers, in the name of our Lord Jesus Christ, that all of you agree with one another so that there may be no divisions among you and that you may be perfectly united in mind and thought" (1 Cor. 1:10). They had discord because they had focused on their religious differences rather than focusing on Christ who made them one body. In his letter to the Philippians, Paul pleaded with Euodia and Syntyche to agree with each other in the Lord. These women had both worked in Paul's ministry, yet there arose such a disagreement between them that Paul had to write to the others in the church to help them mend their disagreement. This shows you can both be dedicated Christians and still struggle with disagreements.

However, God pleads with us in his Word not to let our disagreements divide us so that we cannot accomplish what he has called us to do. Regardless of what you may disagree about, there are some areas where you can agree. Wherever you can agree that touches anything God wants you to accomplish in this life, you have tremendous potential in prayer. You have Jesus' promise that God will hear those prayers and that Jesus will be in your midst whenever you unite in prayer.

Keep in mind that God will never give you anything that disagrees with his Word, even if the two of you agree about it. Think of Scripture as the "music" with which you both can come into harmony as you agree with it. Let God's Word set your hearts to praying together.

You will have more confidence in prayer if you know what you are asking agrees with general things God approves. For example, let's say you pray for God to provide the money you need to take care of your children. Your confidence will be bolstered if you call to mind the verse that says, "I was young and now I am old, yet I have never seen the righteous forsaken or their children begging bread" (Ps. 37:25). So, whenever you can, identify Bible verses that agree with the requests you are making together.

Practice

⧗ Agree together to do the following.

1. Make a list of the things you both can agree about in prayer right now.

2. Pick three items for today; one of you write down those requests.

Prayer Requests We Both Agree On _____

_____

_____

3. Take your agreed-upon requests before the Father in prayer.

- One of you should begin by thanking the Father for his promise that Jesus will be with you when you gather in his name and that he will answer your prayers according to his promises.

- Then speak the requests out loud.

- Have the other follow each request with the words, "Yes, Lord. I agree."

Promises

God's Promise to You
Jesus said, "Again, I tell you that if two of you on earth agree about anything you ask for, it will be done for you by my Father in heaven" (Matt. 18:19).

Your Promise to Each Other
To agree together in prayer whenever you can.

Prayer

Our Father in heaven,

Thank you for giving us each other. Thank you for promising that whenever the two of us come together in Jesus' name, we can count on him being in our midst. Thank you for the promise that if we agree about anything on earth, it will be done for us according to your will because we ask in Jesus' name.

Father, there are times we disagree. Please help us to focus on living our lives in agreement with you and each other more and more. May we make the most of this privilege of prayer by agreeing together as much as possible. Amen!

Day Three

Bless Each Other in Prayer

Purpose

- To consider how we can bless each other according to God's Word

- To learn to pray a blessing over each other

- To bless each other in prayer and through the laying on of hands

Premise

The last thing we see Jesus doing before his ascension is blessing his followers. Luke 24:50–53 says, "When he had led them out to the vicinity of Bethany, he lifted up his hands and blessed them. While he was blessing them, he left them and was taken up into heaven. Then they worshiped him and returned to Jerusalem with great joy. And they stayed continually at the temple, praising God."

Throughout his ministry Jesus laid hands on people and blessed them. Mothers would flock to him, bringing their children to him so that he might lay his hands on them. Mark's Gospel records this scene: "People were bringing little children to Jesus to have him touch them, but the disciples rebuked them. When Jesus saw this, he was indignant. He said to them, 'Let the little children come to me, and do not hinder them, for the kingdom of God belongs to such as these. I tell you the truth, anyone who will not receive the kingdom of God like a little child will never enter it.' And he took the children in his arms, put his hands on them and blessed them" (10:13–16).

The word translated "bless" here also means "to speak well of, invoke a benediction, to praise." To speak a blessing is contrasted with its opposite, cursing, in James 3:10. The word *blessing* means fine speaking, a commendation, praise, eloquence of language. There is a correlation with resting one's hand on the head of another affectionately and blessing another with your words.

You can bless each other in prayer by resting your hand on your partner's head and speaking words of blessing. We see this done throughout the Old Testament. You can do the same for each other using Scripture to speak God's blessing into your lives.

The Bible speaks of many ways that you may invoke a blessing on each other. The Lord taught Moses a blessing the priests were to use to bless the people of Israel. It's found in Numbers 6:22–26 and is commonly used as a benediction today. Paul blessed Timothy (2 Tim. 1:6) by laying hands on him and praying over him for his spiritual gifts. Believers throughout the Book of Acts and the apostles prayed for an outpouring of the Holy Spirit on others by laying hands on them. You too can bless each other by laying on hands and praying for such blessings in your mate's life.

Practice

⧗ Take turns blessing each other in the following ways.

1. Have your partner sit down. Then kneel with your hands on his or her head and pray this blessing: "The LORD bless you and keep you; the LORD make his face shine upon you and be gracious to you; the LORD turn his face toward you and give you peace" (Num. 6:24–26).

2. While your hands are still resting on your partner's head, ask God to bless, protect, guide, and uplift your mate. Thank God for all the good you see in him or her, praising and commending your mate before the Lord.

   Pray for God's blessing to be manifest through the revelation and use of his or her spiritual gifts. If you recognize certain spiritual gifts in your mate, pray for each one specifically, asking that God would open up opportunities for these gifts to be put to good use in his kingdom.

3. Pray that God would bless your mate's life with a fresh in-filling of the Holy Spirit and that he or she would receive power from on high to be a living witness of Jesus to the world.

☒ When you have finished blessing your partner in all these ways, trade places and repeat the process.

Promises

God's Promise to You
"Do not repay evil with evil or insult with insult, but with blessing, because to this you were called so that you may inherit a blessing" (1 Pet. 3:9).

Your Promise to Each Other
To speak blessing into each other's lives and pray that God will bless your mate.

Prayer

Our Father in heaven,

Thank you for the many blessings we enjoy. May your blessing rest upon us both. May we continually bless each other and speak blessing into each other's lives. In Jesus' name. Amen!

Day Four
Fast and Pray Together When Necessary

Purpose

- To learn what the Bible has to say about praying and fasting that relates to your lives

- To identify kinds of situations in which praying and fasting are effective

- To identify specific situations in which fasting and praying together could help

Premise

There will be situations in your lives that call for a greater degree of solidarity in prayer. There are times the two of you may need to engage in praying and fasting together. Fasting—in its various forms—is depriving yourself of something (usually food and drink) while you focus on God for a particular purpose.

At the heart of any biblical fast is the desire to draw closer to God and to do his will. Once when the disciples spoke to Jesus regarding food, he replied, "My food is to do the will of him who sent me and to finish his work" (John 4:34). When we allow our bodies to go hungry, or when we deprive ourselves of something else that we rely on, we are better able to sense the spiritual hunger to do God's will. Fasting can also humble us before God.

In the Old Testament, fasting was a prescribed part of the Jewish religious calendar. It was required at set times, yet—according to Isaiah 58—God still wanted those who fasted to do so with a right attitude. Things changed in the life of the New Testament church; it no longer required strict adherence to Old Testament law. Yet there are accounts of fasting and teaching on fasting in the New Testament that make it clear that it should remain part of the Christian experience.

When Jesus was asked about fasting, he didn't say, "If you fast . . . ," he said, "When you fast. . . ." Consider these words of Jesus to his followers: "When you fast, do not look somber as the hypocrites do, for they disfigure their faces to show men they are fasting. I tell you the truth, they have received their reward in full. But when you fast, put oil on your head and wash your face, so that it will not be obvious to men that you are fasting, but only to your Father, who is unseen; and your Father, who sees what is done in secret, will reward you" (Matt. 6:16–18).

Jesus also said that his followers would fast when the bridegroom—himself—was taken from them. We are his followers but we live in the age when our bridegroom—Jesus—has gone away, and we await his return. Therefore, we should at least understand the role fasting can play in our spiritual lives and be prepared to do so together when it becomes necessary.

Notice that most accounts of fasting in the Bible involve people who agree to fast in order to achieve a specific goal. The following are situations from the Bible that model fasting for us. As you consider each situation, think about whether there might be a similar situation in your lives that could benefit from the two of you agreeing to a time of focused prayer and fasting.

⧗ If time is short, pick one or two of these to read now. You can go back later to consider the rest.

Purpose or Circumstance	People and Scripture Reference
As a part of a life of spiritual devotion	Anna the Prophetess Luke 2:36–38 Daniel and friends Daniel 1:1–16
In life or death situations and times of crisis	King Jehoshaphat at invasion of Judah by three enemy armies 2 Chronicles 20:1–26 Queen Esther learning of planned holocaust of the Jews Esther 4:1–5:2
When special protection was needed	Ezra the priest as Jewish exiles headed home to Jerusalem Ezra 8:21–23

As demonstration of repentance from sin and pleading for God's mercy	King David to spare the life of his child born of sin 2 Samuel 12:1–23 People of Nineveh repenting at Jonah's preaching Jonah 3:1–10
Seeking God for guidance	Church at Antioch before setting apart Paul and Barnabus as missionaries Acts 13:2–3 Paul and Barnabus before appointing elders in the churches Acts 14:23
For spiritual power needed to overcome some kinds of demonic forces that don't otherwise respond to prayer	Jesus casting demon out of boy after disciples could not Mark 9:26–29*

Practice

While you may not be prepared to or even need to proclaim a fast today, there will be times when fasting is something the two of you will need to agree to do together. This practice section will help you prepare yourselves for such situations.

Share with each other any experience you may have already had in your Christian life with fasting. Tell how this practice impacted your spiritual life, what prompted you to fast, and any effects you saw as a result of fasting and praying for a specific purpose.

⌛ Consider the following circumstances that may call for fasting to see if there are examples in your lives that would benefit from a time of fasting together.

List any situation in your lives that constitute a crisis or is a matter of life or death: _____

List any area of sin that has brought terrible consequences on your lives and that is occasion for repentance and seeking God's mercy: _____

_____

*Note that only some manuscripts mention fasting in this verse.

List any situation in which one of you, both of you, a loved one, or a ministry you're involved in needs special divine protection: _____

_____

List areas where either or both of you, or your church, needs direct guidance from God: _____

_____

List any situations where either of you or one of your loved ones seems to be in bondage to spiritual forces of darkness or demonic influences that have not been broken by prayer alone: _____

_____

_____

⧗ Decide together whether you will take up any such situations in praying and fasting. When the time comes to fast, follow these guidelines:

1. Learn more about biblical fasting by reading Isaiah 58, the passages listed in the chart above, and the book *God's Chosen Fast* by Arthur Wallis. If you have health conditions that could be adversely affected by fasting, check with your doctor before you begin.

2. Agree on the purpose of your fast.

3. Agree on a time for the fast. This may be certain hours of the day, a certain day each week for a set period of time, or a certain number of days.

4. Agree on what you will give up for your fast (this could be food, certain kinds of food and drink, or even other things such as TV, negative thinking, and so on).

5. Set aside times to pray together during your fast. (The time you would eat is a good time.)

6. Record all insights God gives you, answers to your prayers regarding your reason for fasting, and any breakthrough in spiritual warfare that occurs during and after your fast. (God will not always do what you want, but when you are fasting, God may help you understand why he is not doing things your way.)

Promises

God's Promise to You

When you fast as God desires (as described in Isaiah 58) God promises: "Then your light will break forth like the dawn, and your healing will quickly appear; then your righteousness will go before you, and the glory of the LORD will be your rear guard. Then you will call, and the LORD will answer; you will cry for help, and he will say: Here am I. . . . Then your light will rise in the darkness, and your night will become like the noonday. The LORD will guide you always; he will satisfy your needs in a sun-scorched land and will strengthen your frame. You will be like a well-watered garden, like a spring whose waters never fail. Your people will rebuild the ancient ruins and will raise up the age-old foundations; you will be called Repairer of Broken Walls, Restorer of Streets with Dwellings" (Isa. 58:8–9a, 10b–12).

Your Promise to Each Other

To be willing to join together in fasting and praying on each other's behalf.

Prayer

Our Father in heaven,

Please help us dare to go deeper in our spiritual lives. If we have never sought you through praying and fasting, help us prepare our hearts for *when* we fast. Please show us if there are areas of our lives or situations confronting us that could be changed for the better by praying and fasting. Lord, please stir up in us a desire to experience all you have for us. Help us to be willing to set aside the desires of our flesh. Help us get to the point where we can agree with Jesus and say, "Our food is to do your will and finish the work you have given us to do." Amen!

Day Five
Pray God's Word over Yourself and Your Mate

Purpose

- To learn how to turn God's Word into prayers, which God promises to answer

- To learn to use something in human nature to spiritual advantage in your prayer life

- To practice praying God's Word for yourself and your mate

Premise

When it comes to having your prayers answered, 1 John 5:14–15 makes an astounding promise. It says, "This is the confidence we have in approaching God: that if we ask anything according to his will, he hears us. And if we know that he hears us—whatever we ask—we know that we have what we asked of him."

The best way to know that God hears your prayers is to be sure you ask according to his will. The Bible is the express will of God. Therefore, if you accurately handle God's Word and ask God to bring about what is written in the Bible, God will hear your prayers and give you what you ask of him.

This understanding forms the basis for praying Scripture, or praying God's Word back to him. This can become an effective way to pray for yourself and for your mate. If you read that the Bible says, "Go into all the world and preach the gospel," you can confidently pray, "Lord, please help me go into all the world and preach the gospel"; or "Please help my husband (or wife) go into all the world and preach the gospel." When you read in the Bible, "Love your neighbor as you love yourself," you can confidently pray, "Lord, help me love my wife (or husband) as I love myself." God already has declared that he wants to answer these prayers. So when you pray them, you can be assured God will respond positively.

This is a fairly simple practice. You just have to make sure that you don't take a verse or Bible promise out of context and use it for your own purposes, which may not be in God's will for you. You have to see who the promise applies to or to whom the admonition is given and make sure that you are not applying it inappropriately. For example, 1 Kings 3:13 records a promise God made to Solomon. It says, "Moreover, I will give you what you have not asked for—both riches and honor—so that in your lifetime you will have no equal among kings." That is God's holy Word telling us what he promised to Solomon.

It would be a misuse of Scripture to pray, "Lord, I pray for you to give me both riches and honor so that in my lifetime I will have no equal." This falls under the category of prayers that will not be answered as described in James 4:3, "When you ask, you do not receive, because you ask with wrong motives, that you may spend what you get on your pleasures."

Sometimes it's easier to pray for your mate than it is to pray for yourself. Lucy Swindoll (sister of Pastor Chuck Swindoll) says her favorite three-word prayer is, "Lord, change them!" While Lucy is not married, she points out something common to human nature that can help you with regard to praying for each other. Human nature is such that we readily see where those closest to us need to change while we hardly notice areas of our own lives that need to be changed by God.

You can use this understanding of human nature to your advantage. This is the same quality Jesus pointed out when he said, "Why do you look at the speck of sawdust in your brother's eye and pay no attention to the plank in your own eye? How can you say to your brother, 'Let me take the speck out of your eye,' when all the time there is a plank in your own eye? You hypocrite, first take the plank out of your own eye, and then you will see clearly to remove the speck from your brother's eye" (Matt. 7:3–5).

We might as well all admit it; it is much easier to read the Bible and see the verses that apply to how others need to change than to reflect on our own lives. Today, we will show you how to use this tendency to actually enhance your prayer life and bless your mate in two different ways.

Practice

1. Read the following verse and think of how you could make it a prayer for your mate: "But the fruit of the Spirit is love, joy, peace, patience, kindness, goodness, faithfulness, gentleness and self-control. Against such things there is no law" (Gal. 5:22–23). If a wife prayed this for her husband, it might go something like this: "Father, I thank you that I see my husband growing in you. By your gracious Spirit, I pray you grow the fruit of your Spirit—love, joy, peace, patience, kindness, goodness, faithfulness, gentleness, and self-control—in his life as he dedicates himself to being filled daily with your Spirit. Amen."

2. Write your prayer for your mate based on this verse on a separate piece of paper. This prayer can get even better if you apply Jesus' advice about not looking at the speck in another's eye without first seeing what is in your own. Before you pray for your mate, proceed to step three.

3. Use Galatians 5:22–23 as a mirror to look into your own eyes and life. This is in keeping with what James 1:23–25 says about using God's Word as a mirror. Here is how you would pray a reflective prayer with the same verse: "Heavenly Father, I want to have the fruit of your Holy Spirit in my life. Please show me how well the fruit of love is growing in my life." Then wait silently before God and allow the Holy Spirit to speak to you and bring things to mind.

   "Lord, where is the joy in my life? Am I a person whose life is characterized by your joy that is to be our strength?" Then wait on the Spirit.

   "Lord, how peaceful am I? Does your peace that passes all understanding really guard my heart and mind?" Again, wait for the Holy Spirit to speak to your heart.

   "How about patience, Lord? Is patience growing in my life? Am I patient with my mate? Am I patient with our children? Would people at work describe me as patient or impatient?" Then wait.

   "Dear Lord, where is the kindness in my life?" Wait and listen.

"Lord, is goodness a quality that is growing in my life as I give more and more of myself over to you?" Wait on the Lord to hear what the Holy Spirit speaks.

"Lord, how am I doing in the area of faithfulness? Am I being faithful to my mate—in the inner person of my heart as well as with my body? Am I being faithful to the commitments I've made? Am I a faithful friend?" Wait.

"Lord, am I a gentle person? Does gentleness describe the way I deal with people?" Wait and listen.

"Lord, am I growing to be more self-controlled?" Wait on the Lord.

Surely, you will experience the Holy Spirit testing your fruit. If the Lord shows you specific areas where you fall short of his will, as revealed in his Word, pray (silently or aloud together) and ask him to attend to this area of your life. This will prepare your heart to pray the same verses into your mate's life.

⧗ 4. Now you are ready to pray in the right spirit. Go back to the prayer you wrote for your mate. Take turns praying your prayers aloud for each other.

If you want to further practice this exercise, use the following prayer to get started. Again, you will pray this for your mate—*after* you reflect on it and pray it for your own life.

"Dear Father, I pray that my mate will receive your instruction (Ps. 78:1). May my partner be sensitive to your gentlest whisper of guidance (Isa. 30:21). Awaken my love morning by morning to listen to you. When you speak, I pray my mate will not be rebellious or draw back from following you fully (Isa. 50:4–5). Amen!"

Promises

God's Promise to You
"This is the confidence we have in approaching God: that if we ask anything

according to his will, he hears us. And if we know that he hears us—whatever we ask—we know that we have what we asked of him" (1 John 5:14–15).

Your Promise to Each Other
To reflect on God's Word as applied to your own life before you pray God's Word over each other's lives.

Prayer

Our Father in heaven,

You have given us a great and precious promise, that whenever we pray according to your will, you will hear and answer us. Please teach us to make the most of this promise. Help us see how we can pray your will for each other, but remind us to first examine our own lives. Please help us to see how your holy Word applies to us before we try to help each other correct anything that does not line up with your Word. Amen!

WEEK FOUR

Get into God's Word Together

Introduction

"In the beginning was the Word, and the Word was with God, and the Word was God." So begins the Gospel of John. The Word of God is God himself expressed for us so that we may know him. Knowing the Word of God gives us an absolute standard of truth, godliness, and conduct. It gives us the promises that God will keep; it gives us guidance, correction, reproof. It gives us all we need for life and godliness. Therefore, it is imperative that the Word of God be at the center of our lives, that we bow together before God and seek to know and obey his will as it is revealed in the Bible's pages.

This week the two of you will have the opportunity to interact with the Word of God in many ways. If you are not familiar with the Bible, don't worry! You can start at your own level of Bible knowledge. What matters most is that you set your heart to receive, believe, and obey God's Word by the power of his Holy Spirit.

Man to Man
with Bill McCartney

Since God is revealed in his Word, the Holy Bible, it is impossible to fully love God without loving his Word. The great psalmist, King David, said this of a man who loves God with all his heart: "His delight is in the law of the Lord, and on his law he meditates day and night. He is like a tree planted by streams of water, which yields its fruit in season and whose leaf does not wither. Whatever he does prospers" (Ps. 1:2–3). This is not the portrait of a lukewarm man. It's the portrait of a man who's *hot* after God. Delighting in the Word of God is not a lukewarm action. A tree planted by streams of water is not just surviving—it's a flourishing, thriving, towering tree. A man who prospers in all he does can't possibly be lukewarm. He's energized, focused, dedicated to the task at hand. That's how you should approach getting into God's Word this week with your wife.

I've learned that I can get more out of God's Word by listening to my wife's perspective. She will pick up on things I overlook, and I do the same for her. Our wives have instincts, insights, and intuitions that serve to give us information we truly need. This will evidence itself as you search Scripture together. Discover how uniquely your wife sees things that complete the picture for you.

Woman to Woman
with Lyndi McCartney

When you first met your husband, didn't you delight in the time you had together getting to know each other? You never would have felt satisfied if you could not have been with him but instead learned about him through what others told you. You would not have felt truly connected. It's the same with getting to know the Lord. An introduction is not knowing him. Reading his Word allows you to get to know his heart, and knowing his heart is what connects you. When you and your husband study God's heart together, you add another dimension to your faith and hearty proportions of love to your marriage. Investigating together enables you to work together for God's glory. Remember, he sees the two of you as one. What could delight the Father more than your presence and hearts set together to seek after him?

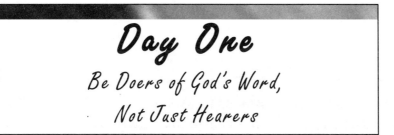

Day One
Be Doers of God's Word,
Not Just Hearers

Purpose

- To encourage each other to be doers of God's Word, not just hearers

- To practice doing God's Word in some way whenever you hear it together

Premise

Being married gives you repeated opportunities to hear God's Word together. Think of all the times you have shared hearing God's Word: through sermons, Bible studies, Christian radio broadcasts and television programs, tapes, discussions. There is no shortage of opportunities to hear God's Word today in our country. However, with the myriad opportunities to hear God's Word, there is increased danger of becoming *mere hearers* of God's Word and not doers. As marriage partners, you can help each other remember not to just hear but also to *respond* to God's Word by doing it.

The Book of James warns, "Do not merely listen to the word, and so deceive yourselves. Do what it says. Anyone who listens to the word but does not do what it says is like a man who looks at his face in a mirror and, after looking at himself, goes away and immediately forgets what he looks like. But the man who looks intently into the perfect law that gives freedom, and continues to do this, not forgetting what he has heard, but doing it—he will be blessed in what he does" (James 1:22–25).

Here God's Word is likened to a mirror that we should use to see what needs to change. Then we should take action based on what we see that is not as it should be. When you look in a mirror, you notice whether your hair is out of place, whether you have anything in your teeth or a bit of mustard on your chin. If you noticed any such thing, you would immediately take action to put yourself back into good shape.

Use God's Word as a basis for a personal checkup; take time to look at yourself and see if your life is matching up to what God's Word says it should be. And if you see something that is spiritually or practically out of place in your life, just seeing it isn't enough. Just hearing what God says isn't enough. In time you will forget. Instead, follow up with immediate action to correct whatever needs to be corrected in your life.

There are two common pitfalls relating to being hearers and not doers of God's Word.

1. Instead of applying God's message to your own life, you critique how well it was presented. This can happen on the drive home after church or at the Sunday meal. The conversation may revolve around how well the preacher presented the sermon or how he compared to someone else. You may discuss what you thought was lacking, or the style of the speaking, or even what the preacher or teacher was wearing.

2. Instead of listening to what God's Word has to say *to you,* you listen to see how it applies to someone else—often your mate. You may find yourself keeping track of the verses that you can use to get your mate to do something. You may even give him or her a nudge or a raised eyebrow as if to say, *Are you listening? This is for YOU!* Or you may take notes of what you think someone else needs to know and change in his or her life.

Avoiding these pitfalls can benefit you greatly. Consider what one couple did. They agreed to find one thing they could *do* in response to each sermon they heard. This brought them several benefits. They found that they were getting something out of church each week. They found that changing what they were looking for caused them to stop criticizing the pastor. They came away from church with a sense that God was moving in their lives. And indeed he was. The key was that they had chosen to become doers of the Word and not just hearers.

It may take self-discipline to get out of these pitfalls, especially if you habitually listen to God's Word in either of these ways. However, if the two of you agree to help each other, you can change your habits. Begin right away to encourage each other to be doers of God's Word and not just hearers. Here's how.

Practice

⚎ 1. Agree together that you will focus your minds on listening to God's Word for the purpose of reflecting on your own lives, no one else's.

⚎ 2. Whenever you hear a sermon or any presentation of God's Word, ask each other, "How did that speak to you?" and "What could we do in response to what we heard?"

⚎ 3. If you hear God's Word and don't notice anything you need to change in your life, praise God! That means the Holy Spirit has already been working in that area of your life. Thank God for his ongoing work within you and the fruit you see.

Test Yourselves
List the topics of all the sermons or Bible studies you have heard over the last month.

Husband	Wife
_____	_____
_____	_____
_____	_____

Are you having trouble remembering some of them? This may be an indication that you were only hearing. If you are not applying what you hear, James says that you go away and immediately forget it.

Of those messages that you can remember, think of specific things you changed because of what you heard. List those changes here.

Husband	Wife
_____	_____
_____	_____
_____	_____

Another thing you can do together is to choose one verse a day to *do*. Then commend each other whenever you notice the Scripture in action. If time is short or you don't want to do this exercise every day, choose one verse to do today. You may want to choose one a week hereafter and try to catch each other doing what the verse says sometime during the week. Here are a few verses to get you started: Ephesians 4:32; Colossians 3:9–10; 1 Thessalonians 5:11; 1 Thessalonians 5:15; James 5:9; James 5:16; 1 Peter 4:8–10; Zechariah 7:9.

Promises

God's Promise to You
"But the man who looks intently into the perfect law that gives freedom, and continues to do this, not forgetting what he has heard, but doing it—*he will be blessed in what he does*" (James 1:25).

Your Promise to Each Other
To agree to look for ways to put any presentation you hear of God's Word into action.

Prayer

Our Father in heaven,

You know us so well! You know we're inclined to listen to your Word without reflecting on our own lives. Lord, forgive us for the times we saw areas of our lives that were out of line with your Word but did nothing about them. Please forgive us for the times we heard your Word but thought only about how it applied to someone else. Forgive us for the times we focused on critiquing the presentation of your Word instead of listening to what you had to say to us.

Lord, we agree that we want to be doers of your Word, not just hearers. Please help us. In Jesus' name. Amen!

Day Two

Read God's Word for Reproof, Correction, and Training in Righteousness

Purpose

- To understand that God's Word is given for teaching, rebuking, correcting, and training in righteousness

- To practice reading God's Word with an open heart, ready to respond to the teaching, rebuking, correcting, and training in righteousness God provides

- To practice responding positively to the reproof, correction, or training in righteousness you find as you read the Bible

Premise

As the two of you go through life together, one goal you can share is to grow in your knowledge of God's Word and let it accomplish God's purposes for your lives. This includes more than memorizing all the books of the Bible, or any particular passage, or a set of Bible facts. God wants to change his relationship with both of you and to change you as you respond to his teachings.

God's goal is not that we would know the Bible for the sake of knowledge. He wants us to experience the fellowship that comes when we become willing to do what he says, dedicate ourselves to knowing his teachings, obey his teachings by the power of the Holy Spirit, and therefore experience close fellowship with the Father and the Son as promised in John 14:23.

Second Timothy 3:16–17 also teaches us that, "All Scripture is God-breathed and is useful for teaching, rebuking, correcting and training in righteousness, so that the man of God may be thoroughly equipped for every good work." Let's consider each of these purposes God wants his Word to accomplish in your life.

Teaching

Teaching is translated in some versions as doctrine. There are basic beliefs, truths, teachings, and revelations in the Old and New Testaments that are foundational to understanding God and his will for humanity. There were true prophets, whose words are recorded in the canon of Scripture. There were and still are false prophets who expound beliefs and teachings that oppose the truths laid out in the Bible. If you don't know what the Bible teaches, what it stands for, and what God forbids, you will not be able to determine whether the beliefs influencing your life are of God or not. What you believe will determine what you do, and what you do will determine what becomes of your life. Therefore, it is vital that every Christian understand and uphold the basic teachings of the Bible.

Rebuking

Some versions translate *rebuking* as reproof, meaning to reveal a fault. It also carries with it a legal connotation of convicting or showing evidence. There will be times you read God's Word and the Holy Spirit will use it to convict you of some fault in your life or point out evidence of some way your life falls short of God's will.

Correcting

Correcting means to straighten up again or put in proper order again. Our lives have a way of continually going from order to disorder. It's like keeping a house in order. Even in a well-furnished and -decorated home, the need to keep putting things back in order remains. This kind of constant straightening up is what God wants to do in us as we read the Bible.

Training in Righteousness

The word translated as training or instruction comes from a root word meaning pathos or suffering. This may seem odd at first, but think about it. When we see the truth about ourselves, especially truth that points out our faults and tells us we need to straighten up—again—that can hurt! But God's goal is not to hurt us, his goal is to equip us for every good work he has planned for us. Understanding that training in righteousness may not always be comfortable will encourage us not to shy away from God's Word when it hurts to face the truth.

Rather, we can prepare ourselves to welcome God's work within us by means of his living Word.

Practice

⧗ For this exercise, you will each read a portion of God's Word silently. As you do, look for God's lessons—for yourself. Make it a game as you search God's Word to find *teaching or doctrine* (a truth or belief that God wants you to know), *reproof* (something that convicts you or points out a fault in your life), *correction* (something that tells you how you need to straighten up or points out some area of your life that has gotten out of order), and *instruction* (something that tells you what you need to do—even though it may hurt!). When you find any of these, record them below.

⧗ 1. Set your heart and mind to be willing to do God's will. (You might say to each other, "I'm willing if you're willing.")

⧗ 2. Pray and ask the Holy Spirit to apply God's Word to your life as you read.

3. Open your Bibles to the Sermon on the Mount found in Matthew 5–7. Silently read these three chapters looking for anything the Holy Spirit brings to your attention in each of the four categories. When you find something you respond to in any category, list it in the corresponding column.

⧗ If time is short, read the passage together, identifying one item in each category.

	Husband	Wife
Teaching	_____	_____
	_____	_____
	_____	_____
Reproof	_____	_____
	_____	_____
	_____	_____

Correction _____   _____

_____   _____

_____   _____

Training _____   _____

_____   _____

_____   _____

Share your lists with each other. Then discuss whether this felt different from simply reading God's Word to fill your quota for the day or for mere head knowledge.

Once you are aware of your faults, where you need to straighten up, and where the truth hurts because it strikes home for you, God wants you to turn to him. He does not convict you without being willing to help you change in these areas. The prayer today will be a prayer each of you compose in response to God's Word.

Promises

God's Promise to You
"Jesus replied, 'If anyone loves me, he will obey my teaching. My Father will love him, and we will come to him and make our home with him'" (John 14:23).

Your Promise to Each Other
Not to use Scripture to point out faults in each other, but to read God's Word with an openness for God to convict you of your own faults and a willingness to change by the power of the Holy Spirit.

Prayer

Take turns transforming your list from the practice section into a prayer by filling in the following blanks.

Our Father in heaven,

Thank you for teaching me _____ (what you

wrote under teaching). When I read the verse about _____ (what you wrote under reproof), I was convicted of a fault in my own life which is _____·_____. As I read the part about _____ (what you wrote under correction), I could see where my life needs to be straightened up again in the area of _____. Lord, I need you to train me in righteousness. Reading the part about _____ (what you wrote under training), I felt it. The truth hurt because it came so close to home, and I know that I am not yet living as right-eously as you would have me. Lord, I am willing to do your will, even though I need the help of your Holy Spirit every day. Please forgive me for falling short in these areas. Please help me become fully equipped for every good work. In Jesus' name. Amen!

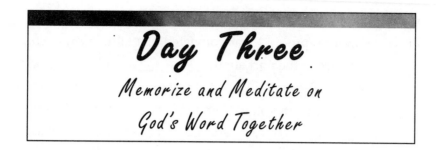

Day Three
Memorize and Meditate on God's Word Together

Purpose

- To understand the power and purpose of memorizing and meditating on God's Word

- To include memorizing and meditating on God's Word as part of your shared devotional life

Premise

Our minds are filled with many things, yet there is nothing that compares with the Word of God. You can help each other spiritually by encouraging and supporting each other in memorizing and meditating on God's Word.

The Lord told Joshua, "Do not let this Book of the Law depart from your mouth; *meditate on it* day and night, so that you may be careful to do everything written in it. Then you will be prosperous and successful. Have I not commanded you? Be strong and courageous. Do not be terrified; do not be discouraged, for the LORD your God will be with you wherever you go" (Josh. 1:8–9).

According to this passage, what purpose was served by Joshua meditating on God's law? _____

_____

What benefit would he receive? _____

Do you think this could apply to you? Do you think that meditating on God's Word day and night would help you be careful to do everything written in it?

_____

Do you think that having your mind filled with God's Word, having a mental storehouse of God's truths and promises, would help you be strong and courageous? _____

Can you think of a time when a particular verse you memorized gave you courage or strength? Share your experiences with each other.

King David extolled the virtues of meditating on God's Word. Psalm 119 speaks of meditating eight times. Note what David was meditating on in each of these verses.

In Psalm 119:15 David meditated on _____.

In Psalm 119:23 David meditated on _____.

In Psalm 119:27 David meditated on _____.

In Psalm 119:48 David meditated on _____.

In Psalm 119:78 David meditated on _____.

In Psalm 119:97 David meditated on _____.

In Psalm 119:99 David meditated on _____.

In Psalm 119:148 David meditated on _____.

David had a goal in mind when he hid God's Word in his heart. Write out Psalm 119:11. _____

_____

_____

You may have noticed that even though David was so committed to memorizing and meditating on God's Word, he still committed grievous sins. This is true, but we don't know how often he was also deterred from sin. The Scripture we memorize not only deters us from sin, but it can also comfort us if we sin. It can assure us of God's steadfast love and his willingness to forgive our sins.

⌛ Think of a time (if you can) when a verse of Scripture you memorized deterred you from sin. (Any of the Ten Commandments counts.) Share this with each other.

In the New Testament we also see that Jesus knew God's Word by heart. Although Jesus was the Word who was made flesh, as a man he was prepared to recite God's Word at appropriate moments. When he was tempted by the devil, he dealt with every temptation by reciting Scripture. And the devil left him! The spoken Word of God has power that we can use to refute the enemy when we are tempted.

Practice

Look up the following verses and take turns reading them aloud to each other. While you read them, keep track of all the different things we are told to think about, meditate on, or remember about the Lord.

⧗ If time is short, choose a few to look at now. You can come back to the rest later.

Scripture Reference	What We Are to Remember or Meditate On
1 Chronicles 16:12–13	
Psalm 63:6	
Psalm 77:11	
Psalm 103:17–18	
Psalm 105:5–6	
Psalm 119:13	
Psalm 119:52	
Psalm 143:5	
Isaiah 46:8–11	

⧗ Together, choose *one* verse of Scripture that is meaningful to both of you and agree to memorize it together. Here's a good way to memorize Scripture.

1. Each of you write the verse down.

2. Read it aloud several times to each other.

3. Have your partner look at the verse while you try to repeat it from memory.

4. Practice until you can recite it, then switch roles until you both can.

5. Recite the verse together.

When you go to bed tonight, direct your mind to meditate on one of the things God's Word says to meditate on. When you arise tomorrow, share with each other what you thought about as you meditated according to God's Word. Share how this can change your perspective and your life.

Promises

God's Promise to You
"If you remain in me and my words remain in you, ask whatever you wish, and it will be given you" (John 15:7).

Your Promise to Each Other
To help each other memorize Scripture and to share the things you meditate on in keeping with God's Word.

Prayer

Our Father in heaven,

Our minds are barraged with so many thoughts. Lord, may we devote our thought-life to you. Thank you for giving us your Word in a form we can carry with us. Thank you for the access we have to your Holy Word and for the mental ability to remember. Please help us not to take this for granted. Instead, help us to hide your Word in our hearts so that we may not sin against you. Lord, may the words of our mouths and the meditations of our hearts be acceptable to you.

Please help us help each other to memorize your words. Help us to direct our thoughts to you each night as we lay down to sleep and to speak of you as we arise in the morning. In Jesus' name. Amen!

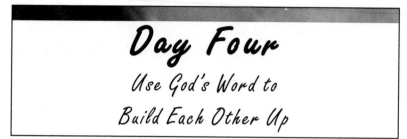

Day Four
Use God's Word to Build Each Other Up

Purpose

- To learn to use God's Word to build up and encourage each other

- To help each other grow in God's love by using his Word to remind each other how much God loves you both

Premise

God calls all Christians to build each other up. When you are married, you have a greater opportunity to build up your mate. Today you will learn some specific ways you can use God's Word to do so. You can use the Word of God as a prayer or benediction (as we did last week). You can take a prayer from Scripture and apply it to your spouse. You can also collect passages of Scripture that are reassuring and have them ready to share with your mate whenever he or she seems to need encouragement. These are not verses for reproof and correction but verses that assure your mate of how great a love God has for him or her.

Practice

⌛ Start today's exercises by praying this prayer from Scripture aloud for your mate. Get on your knees beside your mate, place your hands on him or her, and pray the prayer from Ephesians (see boxed text). When you are finished, trade places. Have your mate get on his or her knees and pray the same prayer for you.

Building Each Other Up by Praying a Prayer from Scripture

I kneel before the Father, from whom his whole family in heaven and on earth derives its name. I pray that out of his glorious riches he may strengthen you with power through his Spirit in your inner being, so that Christ may dwell in your heart[s] through faith. And I pray that you, being rooted and established in love, may have power, together with all the saints, to grasp how wide and long and high and deep is the love of Christ, and to know this love that surpasses knowledge—that you may be filled to the measure of all the fullness of God.

Now to him who is able to do immeasurably more than all we ask or imagine, according to his power that is at work within us, to him be glory in the church and in Christ Jesus throughout all generations, for ever and ever! Amen. (Eph. 3:14–21)

God can actually use you to help answer this particular prayer. You just requested that your mate would (1) be rooted and established in love, (2) have power to grasp how wide and long and high and deep the love of Christ is, and (3) to know this love that surpasses knowledge—that he or she may be filled to the measure of all the fullness of God. This all relates to being fully assured in the love of God. You can help your mate grow in this way by reminding him or her, through the Word of God, of the truth of the love of God.

In some of the following verses, parentheses have been added to show where you may want to insert your mate's name as you apply the verse to him or her. You may want to write these verses in your own handwriting and give them to your mate, or you may want to speak them. But somehow plan to encourage each other with how much God loves and accepts you both.

⧗ These verses are given for current and future use. There is no way to pray through all of them for each other within your agreed-upon time frame today. You may want to choose one to pray for your mate today and look forward to praying others of them for each other in the future.

"No, in all these things we are more than conquerors through him who loved us. For I am convinced that neither death nor life, neither angels nor demons, neither the present nor the future, nor any powers, neither height nor depth, nor anything else in all creation, will be able to separate us from the love of God that is in Christ Jesus our Lord" (Rom. 8:37–39).

"But when the kindness and love of God our Savior appeared, he saved us, not because of righteous things we had done, but because of his mercy. He saved us through the washing of rebirth and renewal by the Holy Spirit, whom he poured out on us generously through Jesus Christ our Savior, so that, having been justified by his grace, we might become heirs having the hope of eternal life" (Titus 3:4–7).

"The LORD appeared to us in the past, saying: 'I have loved you with an everlasting love; I have drawn you with loving-kindness. I will build you up again and you will be rebuilt, (O Virgin Israel). Again you will take up your tambourines and go out to dance with the joyful'" (Jer. 31:3–4).

"For God so loved (the world) that he gave his one and only Son, that whoever believes in him shall not perish but have eternal life. For God did not send his Son into the world to (condemn the world), but to save (the world) through him" (John 3:16–17).

"The Father himself loves you because you have loved me and have believed that I came from God" (John 16:27).

"As he says in Hosea: 'I will call them "my people" who are not my people; and I will call her "my loved one" who is not my loved one'" (Rom. 9:25).

"Be imitators of God, therefore, as dearly loved children and live a life of love, just as Christ loved us and gave himself up for us as a fragrant offering and sacrifice to God" (Eph. 5:1–2).

"Therefore, as God's chosen people, holy and dearly loved, clothe yourselves with compassion, kindness, humility, gentleness and patience" (Col. 3:12).

"May our Lord Jesus Christ himself and God our Father, who loved us and by his grace gave us eternal encouragement and good hope, encourage your hearts and strengthen you in every good deed and word" (2 Thess. 2:16–17).

"This is how God showed his love among us: He sent his one and only Son into the world that we might live through him. This is love: not that we loved God, but that he loved us and sent his Son as an atoning sacrifice for our sins. Dear (friends), since God so loved us, we also ought to love one another. No one has ever seen God; but if we love one another, God lives in us and his love is made complete in us" (1 John 4:9–12).

"To (those) who have been called, who are loved by God the Father and kept by Jesus Christ: Mercy, peace and love be yours in abundance" (Jude 1:1b–2).

"Grace and peace to you from God our Father and the Lord Jesus Christ. Praise be to the God and Father of our Lord Jesus Christ, who has blessed us in the heavenly realms with every spiritual blessing in Christ. For he chose us in him before the creation of the world to be holy and blameless in his sight. In love he predestined us to be adopted as his sons [and daughters] through Jesus Christ, in accordance with his pleasure and will—to the praise of his glorious grace, which he has freely given us in the One he loves. In him we have redemption through his blood, the forgiveness of sins, in accordance with the riches of God's grace that he lavished on us with all wisdom and understanding. And he made known to us the mystery of his will according to his good pleasure, which he purposed in Christ, to be put into effect when the times will have reached their fulfillment—to bring all things in heaven and on earth together under one head, even Christ.

"In him we were also chosen, having been predestined according to the plan of him who works out everything in conformity with the purpose of his will, in order that we, who were the first to hope in Christ, might be for the praise of his glory. And you also were included in Christ when you heard the word of truth, the gospel of your salvation. Having believed, you were marked in him with a seal, the promised Holy Spirit, who is a deposit guaranteeing our inheritance until the redemption of those who are God's possession—to the praise of his glory" (Eph. 1:2–14).

While you are reaffirming God's love, you may also want to reaffirm your own love for your spouse.

Promises

God's Promise to You
"His divine power has given us everything we need for life and godliness through our knowledge of him who called us by his own glory and goodness. Through these he has given us his very great and precious promises, so that through them you may participate in the divine nature and escape the corruption in the world caused by evil desires" (2 Pet 1:3–4).

Your Promise to Each Other
To remind each other of how much God loves you.

Prayer

Our Father in heaven,

Thank you for loving us and for giving us reassurance of your love through the Bible. Lord help us learn to use your Word to build each other up and encourage each other. Please help us remind each other how much you love us. In Jesus' name. Amen!

Day Five

Be Students of God's Word Together

Purpose

- To recommit yourselves to actively study God's Word

- To make plans to study God's Word together as you go through life

- To take a step to begin a fresh effort of studying God's Word

Premise

Second Timothy 2:15 says, "Do your best to present yourself to God as one approved, a workman who does not need to be ashamed and who correctly handles the word of truth."

The King James Version says, "Study to show thyself approved unto God. . . ." You can approach and use God's Word in many ways, but nothing is a substitute for studying God's Word.

It is not enough for Christians to have a casual relationship with God's message to us. We need to handle it accurately—which presumes that we will handle it! The Bible is made up of sixty-six books; each fits into God's overall plan, which has been revealed over the course of fifteen hundred years. If you think of the Bible as a library, instead of thinking of it as one huge and intimidating book, you will be better able to approach studying it.

As a married couple, you have a lifetime to spend together. This gives you the opportunity to set goals to read and study the entire Bible—bit by bit. There are many excellent resources available to help you study God's Word. We live in an age and part of the world where there is a wealth of resources available to us: Bible study classes and meetings in your local church, Bible study workbooks,

books, computer programs, focused groups that promote Bible study (women's groups, men's groups, recovery groups, age-related groups, and so on), radio ministries, community-based Bible study groups (such as Community Bible Study, Precepts, or Bible Study Fellowship), television ministries, para-church organizations (such as Walk Thru the Bible), the Internet, and Christian college classes (many of which can be accessed by computer and pursued from home).

All you need to do is to choose to study the Bible together, decide what part of the Bible you want to start in (with sixty-six books to choose from you're sure to be able to agree on something you both want to study), find a resource to help you, and get started.

Today, we will encourage you to do the following.

1. Evaluate where you each stand in your general knowledge of the Bible.

2. Consider the types of resources available to help you grow in your knowledge of Scripture.

3. Choose some resources that will take you in the direction of getting to know God's Word better.

4. Take one step today that will help you start to study God's Word afresh together.

Practice

Evaluate where you each stand in your general knowledge of the Bible.

⧗ Initial any of the following books of the Bible you have studied (you know what the book is about and who the main characters are). From the Gospels: ___ ___ Matthew, ___ ___ Mark, ___ ___ Luke, ___ ___ John, ___ ___ the Acts of the Apostles; from the letters of the New Testament: ___ ___ Romans, ___ ___ 1 Corinthians, ___ ___ 2 Corinthians, ___ ___ Galatians, ___ ___ Ephesians, ___ ___ Philippians, ___ ___ Colossians, ___ ___ 1 Thessalonians ___ ___ 2 Thessalonians, ___ ___ 1 Timothy ___ ___ 2 Timothy, ___ ___ Titus, ___ ___ Philemon, ___ ___ Hebrews, ___ ___ James, ___ ___ 1 Peter, ___ ___ 2 Peter, ___ ___ 1 John, ___ ___ 2 John, ___ ___ 3 John, ___ ___ Jude, ___ ___ Revelation.

⧗ Initial any of the Old Testament books you have studied. From the five books of the Pentateuch: ___ ___ Genesis, ___ ___ Exodus, ___ ___ Leviticus, ___ ___ Numbers, ___ ___ Deuteronomy; from the twelve historical books of the Old Testament: ___ ___ Joshua, ___ ___ Judges, ___ ___ Ruth, ___ ___ 1 Samuel ___ ___ 2 Samuel, ___ ___ 1 Kings, ___ ___ 2 Kings, ___ ___ 1 Chronicles, ___ ___ 2 Chronicles, ___ ___ Ezra, ___ ___ Nehemiah, ___ ___ Esther; from the five poetical books of the Old Testament: ___ ___ Job, ___ ___ Psalms, ___ ___ Proverbs, ___ ___ Ecclesiastes, ___ ___ Song of Solomon (which has great potential for livening up your love life!); from the five major prophets of the Old Testament: ___ ___ Isaiah, ___ ___ Jeremiah, ___ ___ Lamentations (of Jeremiah), ___ ___ Ezekiel, ___ ___ Daniel; from the twelve minor prophets of the Old Testament: ___ ___ Hosea, ___ ___ Joel, ___ ___ Amos, ___ ___ Obadiah, ___ ___ Jonah, ___ ___ Micah, ___ ___ Nahum, ___ ___ Habakkuk, ___ ___ Zephaniah, ___ ___ Haggai, ___ ___ Zechariah, ___ ___ Malachi.

Don't get discouraged at how few you have initialed! Instead look at all the possibilities and choices before you for studying the Bible together.

Consider the types of resources available to help you grow in your knowledge of Scripture. Think about what kinds of Bible study resources you are both interested in and can agree to pursue together. You may want to review the programs available at your local church, visit a Christian bookstore, or explore the Internet to check out college classes or other on-line Bible study resources.

⧖ You can't do everything at once, but you can do *something* at once! Take one step toward starting your study to show yourselves approved unto God as two who do not need to be ashamed of how you are handling his holy Word. Here are some first steps you can do today to get started.

⧖ If time is short, choose one.

- Call your church office to see what Bible study classes are available and when you could start.

- Call your pastor to see if you could join or start a Bible study group for married couples.

- Drive to the local Christian bookstore.

- Go on the Internet and search for Bible study opportunities and Bible college classes available on-line.

- Look through your bookshelf to see if you already have Bible study resources that the two of you could do together.

- Check the listings in your local phone directory to see if there is a Christian college in your community that would allow you to audit or take a Bible class.

- Call a friend who is a diligent student of God's word and ask for suggestions of good Bible study opportunities in your community.

Choose some resources that will take you in the direction of getting to know God's Word better.

You might need to do more research before you can have your resources in hand. Plan some time this week when you can find some Bible study resources that meet your needs. You may want to talk to your pastor, the proprietor at a Christian bookstore, or people you know who are actively involved in Bible study. When you have chosen a resource (such as a class at church, a guide from a Christian bookstore, an experience like a Walk Thru the Bible seminar), write it here.

The Bible study resource we agree to use together is: _____

_____

Take one step today that will help you start to study God's Word afresh together.

Promises

God's Promise to You
"For everything that was written in the past was written to teach us, so that through endurance and the encouragement of the Scriptures we might have hope" (Rom. 15:4).

Your Promise to Each Other
To set goals to study God's Word together and follow through on those goals as an ongoing part of your married life.

Prayer

Our Father in heaven,

Thank you for sending us your holy Word. Please forgive us for the times we have neglected to study your Word while we filled our minds with other things.

Please help us both to study to show ourselves approved by you. Help us become workmen who handle your Word accurately. Please guide us as we consider the options we have to study the Bible. Help us choose a resource that we can understand and enjoy studying. If there are groups in our church that could help us, please lead us to the right group. If you would have us start a Bible study group for couples in our church, please make that clear.

Lord, as we take the first steps to study the Bible, please help us to encourage each other, so that we might please you together in this way. Amen!

WEEK FIVE

Engage in Spiritual
Warfare Together

Introduction

What would it mean for you to have a lifelong spiritual ally with whom you could confidently face all of life's battles? Imagine having the support of someone standing behind you in prayer and affirming God's grace in your life whenever you had to face a foe. Imagine having a reliable spiritual partner with whom you could share the battles you face together—for the good of your home, children, marriage, health, and financial stability—or those that arise in your shared community, church, and various moral situations. Imagine being free to share your inner struggles with your mate, knowing you would be safe to honestly relate times you cry out like the Apostle Paul, "I do not understand what I do. For what I want to do I do not do, but what I hate I do."

How would your life and spiritual impact improve if the two of you knew you were not only marriage partners but also soldiers in the same unit in God's army, occupying this earthly territory until he returns, advancing the kingdom of God? What if you also joined forces to fully use the power afforded those who come together in Jesus' name—assured that Jesus gives you his spiritual authority as the One who "disarmed the powers and authorities" and "made a public spectacle of them, triumphing over them by the cross" (Col. 2:15)?

Your Christian marriage and your willingness to be sold out to God together gives you the opportunity to develop such an alliance. As with any military preparation, it will take obedience to God's orders, rigorous practice, and devotion to each other in the battles of life. You can start today.

Man to Man
with Bill McCartney

This is war! No one has the prerogative to stay out of the fray. The enemy seeks to divide and destroy. He shouts, Independence! Rights! The Holy Spirit whispers, Interdependence. Obedience to God. Self-sacrifice. Can you discern the voices? God wants men and women who will form units of two to do battle, to occupy earth until Jesus returns, to advance the kingdom of God. To do this we must prepare ourselves, commit ourselves, and practice the drills necessary to equip us to win the spiritual war taking place all around us.

Woman to Woman
with Lyndi McCartney

Feeling safe is a huge thing for most women. Perhaps this is why some of us shy away from learning about spiritual warfare. I remember feeling uncomfortable with the subject of spiritual warfare earlier in my walk with the Lord. I really hated to hear people talk about it. I thought, *Why would anyone give the devil so much time and attention?* Well, spiritual warfare is real and each of us needs to be aware and prepared for the battles we face every day. What is spiritual warfare? This week's lessons will teach you if you don't already know. It will remind you, if you do. What we must always remember is that we don't do battle on our own. Jesus fights for each of us day and night. I'm sure there are so many times he has protected us that we don't realize because—by his grace—nothing bad has happened. But when we learn to take part in our spiritual battles, we grow up to join Jesus in protecting our own lives and each other.

I thank God for those who have prayed for me and conducted spiritual warfare on my behalf. Though great healing has taken place inside of me, I will never be free of the need for my husband's prayers and spiritual warfare on my behalf. None of us dare live without such spiritual covering, which includes the prayers of family and friends on our behalf. So, too, I am learning to take my role in spiritual warfare on behalf of others seriously. My husband is out on the front lines every day, and it is my awesome privilege to do battle through prayer for him many times through the days and nights. When you are doing spiritual battle daily for your husband, you will find that you are less inclined to do battle with him when he comes home.

Day One
Stop Fighting Each Other; Start Fighting Spiritual Forces Arrayed Against You

Purpose

- To recognize the spiritual context in which you live out your marriage and your individual lives

- To be aware of Satan's schemes, so he doesn't outwit you in your spiritual battles

- To stop fighting each other and, instead, stand together as allies when dealing with life's problems, conflicts, and struggles

Premise

The Bible makes it clear that all Christians live in the context of a spiritual battle. We are not asked if we would like to join the battle. When we became Christians, we joined forces with Jesus Christ in a battle that has raged since before the creation of the world. God has given us instructions for prevailing in spiritual battles, but first we must have a basic understanding of the nature of these battles, the nature of our enemy, and his intentions toward us.

When the two of you understand the spiritual context in which your marriage plays out, you will be better prepared to unite against the true enemy of your souls instead of fighting against each other.

The sides are drawn. On one side we have our Holy God: God the Father, our Lord Jesus Christ, and the Holy Spirit; all the holy angels; and all who have come into God's kingdom by the blood of Jesus Christ. On the other side is Satan and the fallen angels and those who are under the power and deception of the evil one. Spiritual awareness of our enemy is not to be reserved for special occasions or times of crisis. The Lord's Prayer, which Jesus taught us, includes both petition for daily bread and the prayer that God "deliver us from evil." Spiritual battles are everyday occurrences. Therefore, your marriage and shared spiritual experience should include standing together against the enemy of your souls—and your marriage—on a daily basis.

There are a few basics of spiritual warfare.

1. Know your enemy! Often you will find yourselves thinking you are fighting against people, perhaps even each other; but Ephesians 6:10–12 says, "Finally, be strong in the Lord and in his mighty power. Put on the full armor of God so that you can take your stand against the devil's schemes. *For our struggle is not against flesh and blood, but against the rulers, against the authorities, against the powers of this dark world and against the spiritual forces of evil in the heavenly realms.*" If you can be confused into fighting against each other, instead of fighting together against your true enemy, you may end up doing damage to those on the Lord's side. You could even wound each other with "friendly fire" while being distracted from your true enemy.

2. Know your enemy's intentions! First Peter 5:8 says, "Your enemy the devil prowls around like a roaring lion looking for someone to devour." Jesus also said, "The thief comes only to steal and kill and destroy; I have come that they may have life, and have it to the full" (John 10:10). Second Timothy 2:26 shows that Satan intends to bring you into bondage, describing those who "escape from the trap of the devil, who has taken them captive to do his will."

3. Know your enemy's schemes! The Bible says that you are to "put on the full armor of God so that you can take your stand against the devil's schemes." Paul said he was not "unaware of Satan's schemes" (2 Cor. 2:11). The word *schemes* denotes a pattern of thought, a plan that is in keeping with the nature and intentions of the one doing the planning— in this case Satan and the forces of darkness. Therefore, in order to be on the alert against your adversary, you need to practice becoming aware of the schemes that grow out of his nature and intentions. When you do

this, you can alert each other to possible dangers and help each other counteract them.

Practice

Study the following chart. Look up the examples in Scripture that show Satan's nature and the verses that show what can counteract his schemes.

⧖ If time is too short, just read the lists of Satan's nature and his schemes. When you get time, go into the Bible for your own verification.

Satan's Nature	Schemes	Example from Scripture	Truth to Counteract Satan
Deceiver / father of lies	Deception	John 8:44; Revelation 12:9; John 14:6;	John 14:6; Jesus is the truth!
Rebel	Division	Separated Adam and Eve from each other; separated humanity from God	2 Corinthians 5:18–21; We have been reconciled to God and called to the ministry of reconciliation
Discourager	Discouragement; uses fear to try to take captives	Hebrews 2:14–15; Nehemiah 4:1–23; 2 Kings 18:19–35	1 Thessalonians 5:11; Encourage each other
Accuser of believers	Brings disgrace; brings condemnation	Revelation 12:10; Job 2:9–10	Luke 6:37; Romans 5:15–19, 8:1–4; Affirm the grace of God; don't condemn each other

Abuser	Uses people to do his dirty work, can work through friends or foes	Matthew 16:22–23, Peter; Luke 22:3–4, Judas; Job 2:9–10; Job's wife	Romans 6:12–13; Ephesians 6:10–12; Don't let Satan use you; give yourself to God; fight spiritual forces, not people being used

Using the chart, you can become aware of Satan's schemes and take a stand on the Lord's side to accomplish God's good purposes in each other's lives. Consider how you can align yourself with God's intentions by dealing with each other in ways that counteract Satan's schemes: honesty instead of deception, unity (closeness) instead of division, encouragement instead of discouragement, extending God's grace and forgiveness to each other instead of condemnation, not allowing for any abuse, and not allowing the enemy of your souls to use you against each other in any way.

⧗ If you are convicted by the Holy Spirit about any time you have been dishonest, deceptive, rebellious, divisive, discouraging, condemning, or abusive to your spouse, take the following action. (1) Confess it to the Lord and your mate, (2) repent—make a decision not to continue and turn from those ways, (3) ask God's forgiveness, (4) receive forgiveness from God and your mate, (5) willingly accept the consequences of your actions, (6) unite to thank God that he has "rescued us from the dominion of darkness and brought us into the kingdom of the Son he loves, in whom we have redemption, the forgiveness of sins" (Col. 1:13–14), and (7) share your commitment with a few other believers to whom you will hold yourself accountable in this specific area.

⧗ You may notice that you find yourself drawn into fights with each other when you mean to come together for God's purposes—like when you meet to do this workbook. Don't be unaware! If you find yourselves drawn into a fight against each other, stop. Pray together. Ask God to help you unite to deal with the problem rather than squaring off against each other.

Promises

God's Promise to You
"You, dear children, are from God and have overcome them, because the one who

is in you is greater than the one who is in the world" (1 John 4:4).

Your Promise to Each Other
To be on the alert to stop fighting against each other and unite to fight together against the enemy of your souls.

Prayer

Our Father in heaven,

Thank you for delivering us out of Satan's kingdom of darkness and transferring us into your kingdom. Lord, help us to remain aware of the devil's schemes so he does not outwit us. We live in a world that is much more prone to deception and darkness than to truth and light. We pray that you will help us be truthful and walk in the light. All around us we see division and separation—within and between churches, between different races, even between us at times. Lord, please use us to counteract this. Please start by bringing us into unity with each other. Use us to bring unity in our church family, unity in the larger body of Christ, and reconciliation between races and other groups who have been divided by the enemy of our souls. When we see each other discouraged, cause us to encourage each other. Lord, please help us never to disgrace, condemn, or abuse each other in any way. If we have done this in the past, convict our hearts and help us to repent. Change our hearts and our ways. Lord, please show us how to extend your grace to each other and to assure each other of your forgiveness and never-ending love. In Jesus' name. Amen!

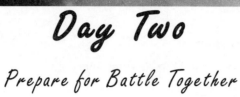

Day Two

Prepare for Battle Together

Purpose

- To learn how to prepare for spiritual battle according to God's Word

- To determine to stand firm together in times of spiritual attack

- To help each other put on and use the spiritual armor and weapons God provides

Premise

Over and over again we are told to live our lives "on the alert" against our enemy. We are told that God has given us armor. We are to wear it, know how to use the shield to fend off the "flaming arrows" of the evil one, and learn to wield the "sword of the Spirit," which is the Word of God. The battle is ongoing, so we're told to suit up. God is our Commander-in-Chief. He expects us to follow his orders, use the protection he provides, and stand firm! Today, you'll consider how to obey these instructions together.

The Roman soldier, whose armor was used as the metaphorical model for ours, did not operate alone. He was part of a unit, and so are you. At the most basic level, you are united as a married couple. Then you are united to those in your family and local church. Together you make up part of the larger body of Christ. The Roman soldier—as is any soldier—was trained in the ideology of his commander, prepared mentally to achieve his mission. We too are expected to become well versed in the ideology and truths of the Bible, which reveals God's mission. The elementary principles of the Bible and God's commanding truths are to govern our actions. Jesus gave us this mission statement as he left earth: "All authority in heaven and on earth has been given to me. Therefore go and make disciples of all nations, baptizing them in the name of the Father and of the Son and of the Holy Spirit, and teaching them to obey everything I have commanded you. And surely I am with you always, to the very end of the age" (Matt. 28:18–20). He is the commander; we are to become disciples and make disciples. We are to discipline ourselves to obey everything that he has commanded us.

Practice

In the context of this military model, the two of you are in the same unit and can help each other remain on the alert against the enemy. You can remind each other to regularly put on the armor God provides. You can help each other learn to use your swords and shields. Below is an exercise to help you do this.

⧗ Consider the following passage of Scripture. Then do the exercises that follow together.

The Full Armor of God

Therefore put on the full armor of God, so that when the day of evil comes, you may be able to stand your ground, and after you have done everything, to stand. Stand firm then, with the *belt of truth* buckled around your waist, with the *breastplate of righteousness* in place, and with your feet fitted with the *readiness that comes from the gospel of peace.* In addition to all this, take up the *shield of faith,* with which you can extinguish all the flaming arrows of the evil one. Take the *helmet of salvation* and the *sword of the Spirit, which is the word of God.* And pray in the Spirit on all occasions with all kinds of prayers and requests. With this in mind, be alert and always keep on praying for all the saints. (Eph. 6:13–18)

This passage of Scripture may be familiar to you, but have you made sure that you understand the spiritual truths it represents? Have you gone further so that you are actually prepared for spiritual warfare in the way the metaphor suggests? Let's start by simply having you make the connection between the various pieces of armor and their spiritual equivalents. Fill in each blank with the correct word found in the verses above. As you do, take time to discuss and consider why each particular association is made.

1. The belt of _____ buckled around your waist.

2. The breastplate of _____ in place.

3. Your feet fitted with the readiness that comes from _____.

4. The shield of _____ with which you can extinguish all the flaming arrows of the evil one.

5. The helmet of _____.

6. The sword of the Spirit, which is _____.

⌛ Consider each piece of armor. Then think of one way you can help each other "put on" or use what each piece of armor is meant to model in your spiritual life. If time is short, read the opening paragraphs but only discuss those questions that are immediately relevant. You can always check off the ones you have talked about and use the others for discussions in the future.

The Belt of Truth

⌛ The soldier's belt held the other pieces of armor together. If the belt was missing, everything else fell apart. This shows that truth is essential to all the other pieces of your spiritual armor.

Consider or discuss: What could you do to help each other know the truth of God's Word? Are you confident that the Bible is the absolute truth? If not, what could the two of you do together to become more knowledgeable and confident in the truth of God's Word? How could you better maintain truthfulness in your relationship with each other? Discuss how a lack of truthfulness endangers soldiers fighting side by side in battle and how a lack of truthfulness between you impairs your ability to stand firmly together in life's battles.

The Breastplate of Righteousness

⌛ The breastplate covered the heart and vital organs. The Bible associates this with righteousness, which is vital to our spiritual life. But it is the righteousness of Jesus that covers us. If we are trusting in our own righteousness, we are left unprotected in a vital area.

Consider or discuss: How confident are you that the righteousness of Jesus covers all your sins? (See Rom. 1:16–17.)

Read Romans 3:21–26 together. According to this passage, what is the basis of your righteousness? _____

_____

Preparation to Go Forth with the Gospel

⌛ Our battle is not merely defensive. We are to "go into all the world and preach the gospel."

Consider or discuss: How have you prepared to share the gospel with others? How can you help each other be prepared to share the gospel with someone else?

The Shield of Faith

⌛ The use of flaming arrows suggests that the attacks of the enemy were designed to damage more than one person at a time. When enemies shot flaming arrows, they intended to set homes or entire towns on fire. The Roman soldier's shield was designed so it could be held next to the shields of other soldiers to form an impenetrable wall. When enemies attacked with flaming arrows, the soldiers banded together to shield the greater community from the flames.

Consider or discuss: How can you unite in your faith to protect your children from the influences of the world that continually bombard them? How can you unite to protect your home? How can you unite to help protect your community from what is unholy and demonic and threatens to destroy what is good and pure in life?

The Helmet of Salvation

⌛ The helmet covered the head—preserving life and metaphorically covering the mind. So, too, you must cover your mind with the assurance of salvation you have received in Jesus Christ. Acts 4:12 says, "Salvation is found in no one else, for there is no other name under heaven"—except the name of Jesus—"given to men by which we must be saved."

Consider or discuss: Do you know that you have salvation through Jesus Christ? If so, reassure each other with God's promises whenever necessary.

The Sword of the Spirit, Which Is the Word of God

The only offensive weapon God provides in this picture is the sword of the Spirit, which is the Word of God. Repeatedly we saw Jesus speak the Word of God to fend off the devil when he was being tempted. Jesus also spoke the word of God with authority to proclaim God's message. And he claimed God's promises. In all these ways he advanced God's kingdom using the "sword of the Spirit."

Consider or discuss: How can you encourage each other to use the Word of God to fend off temptation or advance the kingdom of God? Think of one specific verse of promise from the Bible either of you could use in dealing with a current area of temptation. Practice looking for ways you can use Scripture in dealing with every spiritual battle.

Promises

God's Promise to You

"Submit yourselves, then, to God. Resist the devil, and he will flee from you" (James 4:7).

Your Promise to Each Other

To help each other regularly practice putting on the whole armor of God so that you can stand firm against the enemy together.

Prayer

Our Father in heaven,

You told us to "pray in the Spirit on all occasions with all kinds of prayers and requests." And, "with this in mind, be alert and always keep on praying for all the saints." Lord, please help us begin by praying for each other in every spiritual battle. May we learn to truly live as your soldiers, always on the alert. Help us understand how to put on the full armor of God. Please help us to help each other put on truth and live with the kind of integrity that holds everything else together. Help us trust completely in your righteousness and to put on righteousness. Please help us prepare ourselves to go out to share the gospel with others. May we lift up our faith not only to shield ourselves but also to protect our home, family, church, and community from the fiery attacks of the evil one. Please cover our minds with the assurance of our salvation, based on knowing that Jesus has saved us. Show us how to take up your Word and use it to fend off temptation, claim your promises, and act with the authority you have given us. Lord, please let this illustration be more than words. Make us good soldiers in your army. Help us to stand firm together against the attack of the enemy and fulfill your mission. In Jesus' name. Amen!

Day Three

Unite to Fight Your Shared Spiritual Battles

Purpose

- To learn how to fight shared spiritual battles according to a biblical model

- To identify the shared spiritual battles you are currently facing

- To follow the model in fighting your shared spiritual battles together

Premise

Second Chronicles gives an excellent model for facing a spiritual battle you share with others in God's kingdom. The example concerns King Jehoshaphat of Judah, a good king whom God honored and established. His heart was devoted to the Lord. He tore down the idols and sent teachers throughout Judah to teach the people God's law. He made mistakes, like when he went into battle as an ally of the evil King Ahab and incurred God's displeasure. But afterward, he came home, rededicated himself to God, and worked to turn his people back to the Lord. He set up honest judges and priests to administer justice according to the law of the Lord and to warn the people not to sin.

After this Jehoshaphat and the people of Judah were faced with a serious external threat. Three separate armies joined forces to come against the nation of Judah. You can read the full account in 2 Chronicles 20, but below you have a model of what Jehoshaphat did, along with the verses where you can read the account for yourself.

1. He recognized the danger coming against him and his people (2 Chron. 20:2).

2. He was alarmed, resolved to inquire of the Lord, and proclaimed a fast (2 Chron. 20:3).

3. He gathered his people together to seek help from the Lord (2 Chron. 20:4).

4. He prayed a prayer with these parts:

   - He prayed a prayer that reminded them of God's greatness and power (2 Chron. 20:6).

   - He prayed a prayer that reminded them of previous victories (2 Chron. 20:7).

   - He prayed a prayer recalling God's promises that applied to them (2 Chron. 20:9).

   - He described the problem facing them (2 Chron. 20:10–11).

   - He pointed out how the enemy was undermining God's purposes (2 Chron. 20:11).

   - He asked God to judge the forces arrayed against them (2 Chron. 20:12).

   - He admitted that they were powerless apart from God's power (2 Chron. 20:12).

   - He admitted that they didn't know what to do (2 Chron. 20:12).

   - He said, "But our eyes are upon you" (2 Chron. 20:12).

   - He assembled the whole body in families to pray before the Lord (2 Chron. 20:13).

   - He listened to the Lord when guidance came and obeyed him (2 Chron. 20:15–30).

   - He led his people forward in worship, praise, and thanksgiving—as an act of faith before the victory was won here on earth (2 Chron. 20:20–22).

Practice

The two of you can practice joining together to face a shared spiritual battle using Jehoshaphat's model.

⧗ Think of a spiritual battle that is coming against you both. This wouldn't be something one of you is facing in work or your individual pursuits. Neither would it be an internal battle. Think of something that threatens you on a shared front: the well-being of your marriage, children, home, family, finances, ministry, or something else you share together. It might be a particular problem with a child, a problem in your marriage relationship, some situation in your church that involves you both, dealing with a financial problem (like being in debt or being investigated by the IRS). You may not be facing the kind of intense crisis that Jehoshaphat faced, but choose some shared battle or struggle so that you can practice this kind of spiritual warfare in a non–life threatening situation.

⧗ Now follow the model given by Jehoshaphat.

1. The shared spiritual battle we will address in this exercise is:

   _____

2. Recognize the danger coming against you. What is at stake in this battle?

   _____

3. a) Pray together asking God for guidance and wisdom from above. List any ideas you have as to how the Lord would have you deal with this battle together. Make sure all these plans are in keeping with biblical commands or principles.

   b) Decide whether you should fast. Do you feel this battle is serious enough to warrant a fast? _____ If so, what kind of fast will you do together and for how long? _____

4. Seek help from the Lord together. Hold hands and address the Lord. Tell him that you are gathering in Jesus' name for guidance on this particular problem.

5. Use the following spaces to compose your prayer according to Jehoshaphat's model. When you get to the end of today's exercises, use that time to pray the prayer you will compose here.

⧗ If time is short, list only one thing for each of the following. You may also choose to speak your comments aloud to each other instead of writing them down.

- Compose a few lines that remind you of God's greatness and power. List a few things that are true about God that reminds you that you are praying to God Almighty. (You may want to copy 2 Chronicles 20:6 here.)

  _____

  _____

  _____

- Compose a few lines that remind you of previous victories God has wrought. Recall victories God has won for your family as well as victories in the Bible. _____

  _____

  _____

- Compose a few lines that recall any of God's promises that apply to your situation. _____

  _____

  _____

  _____

  If you cannot think of any that apply to your particular situation, cite Jesus' promise to be with you whenever two or three are gathered in his name and 1 John 5:14–15. (As you become more adept at spiritual warfare you will want to collect promises from God's Word to use in prayer for various kinds of situations. This is one way to use the sword of the Spirit, which is the Word of God, in spiritual battle together.)

⧗ • Describe the problem facing the two of you to the Lord. _____

  _____

  _____

  _____

⧗ • Point out any ways the enemy is using this situation to undermine God's purposes in your lives. _____

  _____

- ⧗ • Ask God to judge anyone involved—and confess if you have been judging them (instead of leaving that to God). _____

  _____

  _____

  _____

- ⧗ • Compose a few lines to admit that you are powerless to deal with this successfully apart from God's power. _____

  _____

  _____

  _____

- ⧗ • Compose a few lines that admit that you don't know what to do, but that your eyes are on the Lord. _____

  _____

  _____

  _____

- • If this spiritual battle involves your entire family or even your church, plan a time to assemble the whole body—in families—to pray before the Lord.

- ⧗ • Be prepared to listen for God's guidance and to obey anything the Lord leads you to do. Note that God will never "impress" you to do something that does not agree with the Bible. Seek guidance from spiritual leaders, such as your pastor. Study God's Word as it relates to your situation and obey all you can find that is applicable. Look for providential circumstances that agree with God's Word, your own higher judgment, guidance from godly counselors, the inner leading of the Holy Spirit (but only if it agrees with the Bible).

- ⧗ • End your prayer with a few lines of worship, praise, and thanksgiving.

  _____

  _____

  _____

  _____

Promises

God's Promise to You
"The angel of the LORD encamps around those who fear him, and he delivers them" (Ps. 34:7).

Your Promise to Each Other
To face your shared spiritual battles together according to guidance given by God through his Word.

Prayer

Go back to the prayer you just composed and pray through it together. When God answers your prayer and helps you win this spiritual battle, record how he gave you victory and the date it occurred. You may find that you have several small victories over little battles associated with the larger one. Keep track of your victories here. _____

_____

_____

_____

_____

_____

Day Four
Become a Spiritual Ally in Your Mate's External Battles

Purpose

- To identify external spiritual battles you each currently face

- To become actively engaged as spiritual allies in each others' external battles

- To practice giving spiritual backup and support for your mate as he or she goes out to fight spiritual battles

Premise

While the two of you will share some of life's battles, there are some spiritual battles you will each face independently. These would be situations in your individual spheres of responsibility, such as at work, in relationships with friends, relationships with members of your extended family, or other situations that do not actively involve you both. These could be struggles related to what Scripture tells us is the influence of the world: "the cravings of sinful man, the lust of his eyes and the boasting of what he has and does" (1 John 2:16).

God does not call you to live each other's lives. There will be battles each of you must face on your own in your individual areas of responsibility in life. However, you can still act as spiritual allies. Scripture says, "Carry each other's burdens, and in this way you will fulfill the law of Christ" (Gal. 6:2). But it also says, "Each one should test his own actions. Then he can take pride in himself, without comparing himself to somebody else, for each one should carry his own load" (Gal. 6:4–5). The "burdens" described in verse 2 refer to an overwhelming weight or situation that no one could bear alone; whereas "his own load" refers to something like a backpack that each individual must carry alone. It describes personal responsibilities that we must each accept as our own. Therefore, God is not calling you to interfere in your mate's work responsibilities or other individual responsibilities. Rather, you can supply spiritual support when it is not appropriate to take direct action in a situation that is not your responsibility.

Practice

⚅ Identify a situation for each of you where you have to deal with a struggle, a difficult situation, a difficult person, an enemy, or other battle that is not directly your mate's business or responsibility. Choose something that is not a shared battle or an inner struggle. Some examples might be having to deal with an ex-spouse, confronting something that is morally wrong in your workplace, repairing a broken relationship with a friend, negotiating a deal, trying to get a raise at work, confronting someone who has wronged you, and so on.

⚅ Take turns listening to each other as you describe your most pressing external battle in which you would like to have your mate as a spiritual ally.

List your external battles here.

Husband: _____

_____

Wife: _____

_____

⚅ Are you willing to commit yourself to enter the spiritual battle in prayer on your mate's behalf? (This means that you will take on this issue as a matter of prayer, consideration, and reflection until the Lord resolves the situation or gives your mate closure regarding the situation. This will also involve listening to your spouse so that you can pray with insight on his or her behalf.) Husband: _____ Wife: _____

⚅ Again you will adapt the model for spiritual warfare drawn from the example of Jehoshaphat in 2 Chronicles 20. This time you will interview each other to compose prayers that you can use to enter the spiritual battles as allies on each other's behalf. Use the following spaces to compose your prayers for your mate. When you get to the end of today's exercises, use that time to pray these prayers.

⧖ If time is short, you can pray each section as you go along without writing your comments out in advance. However, writing helps to solidify and clarify your aims in spiritual warfare to help you remember exactly what you are praying for each other.

⧖ *Husband's Prayer for His Wife's External Battle*

- Compose a few lines that remind you of God's greatness and power.

  _____

  _____

  _____

- Compose a few lines that remind you of previous victories God has wrought in your wife's life.

  _____

  _____

  _____

- Recall or find one of God's promises that applies to your wife's situation.

  _____

  _____

  _____

- Describe the problem facing your wife to the Lord. Recount this first verbally to her to make sure you understand the situation she shared with you. Then write it here.

  _____

  _____

  _____

  _____

  _____

- Point out how the enemy is using this situation to undermine God's purposes in your wife's life.

  _____

  _____

  _____

- Ask God to judge and deal with the forces coming against her—spiritual forces as well as those people who may be mistreating her.

  _____

  _____

  _____

  If you have been judging them, confess it and turn that over to the righteous judge.

- Admit that you are powerless to deal with this situation directly on your wife's behalf and ask God to do what you cannot do.

  _____

  _____

  _____

- Admit that you don't know what to do, but that your eyes are on the Lord.

  _____

  _____

  _____

- Ask God to give your wife wisdom, power, and protection as she deals with this situation apart from you. Ask God to give you compassion and wisdom to know what you can do to help without crossing the boundary of appropriate involvement in her responsibilities.

  _____

  _____

  _____

  _____

  _____

  _____

Wife's Prayer for Her Husband's External Battle

- Compose a few lines that remind you of God's greatness and power.

  _____

  _____

  _____

- Compose a few lines that remind you of previous victories God has wrought in your husband's life.

  _____

  _____

  _____

- Recall or find one of God's promises that applies to your husband's situation.

  _____

  _____

  _____

- Describe the problem facing your husband to the Lord. Recount this first verbally to him to make sure you understand the situation he shared with you. Then write it here.

  _____

  _____

  _____

  _____

- Point out how the enemy is using this situation to undermine God's purposes in your husband's life.

  _____

  _____

  _____

  _____

- Ask God to judge and deal with the forces coming against him—spiritual forces as well as those people who may be mistreating him.

  _____

  _____

  _____

  If you have been judging them, confess it and turn that over to the righteous judge.

- Admit that you are powerless to deal with this situation directly on your husband's behalf and ask God to do what you cannot do.

  _____

  _____

  _____

- Admit that you don't know what to do, but that your eyes are on the Lord.

  _____

  _____

  _____

- Ask God to give your husband wisdom, power, and protection as he deals with this situation apart from you. Ask God to give you compassion and wisdom to know what you can do to help without crossing the boundary of appropriate involvement in his responsibilities.

  _____

  _____

  _____

  _____

Promises

God's Promise to You

"Two are better than one, because they have a good return for their work" (Eccles. 4:9).

Your Promise to Each Other

To continue to provide spiritual support and prayer for these external battles on each other's behalf, and to listen to each other compassionately about these matters until God brings victory or resolves the battles.

Prayer

Take turns praying the prayers you have composed for each other.

Purpose

- To recognize that every person has inner spiritual battles that must be fought

- To understand the basic characteristics of the inner battles every person must fight

- To learn how to engage in spiritual warfare regarding your mate's inner battles

- To join in spiritual warfare for your mate's inner battles

Premise

Every human being has inner battles that must be fought. The outcomes of these inner battles have a direct effect on your marriage, family, success in life, reputation, and spiritual progress. Therefore, these battles can strike fear in you when you consider the possible ramifications of your mate's losing his or her battles within.

Seeing the depravity of one's own sinful nature can be quite shameful and frightening, so people often keep this hidden—even from their mates. And many people would rather believe their mate is so spiritual that he or she is exempt from such inner battles. While this is not biblically correct, it allows them to avoid confronting the depth of the inner struggles their mate may be facing.

Even though these inner battles can be quite disturbing when revealed, the grace of God and our Lord Jesus Christ provides the antidote for the depravity of human nature. When the inner battles rage—as they do even for devoted Christians like the Apostle Paul—you need not be surprised and dare not shy away from these battles. You can be of great support to your mate when he or she is facing such inner turmoil.

The Inner Battle

We know that the law is spiritual; but I am unspiritual, sold as a slave to sin. I do not understand what I do. For what I want to do I do not do, but what I hate I do. And if I do what I do not want to do, I agree that the law is good. As it is, it is no longer I myself who do it, but it is sin living in me. I know that nothing good lives in me, that is, in my sinful nature. For I have the desire to do what is good, but I cannot carry it out. For what I do is not the good I want to do; no, the evil I do not want to do—this I keep on doing. Now if I do what I do not want to do, it is no longer I who do it, but it is sin living in me that does it.

So I find this law at work: When I want to do good, evil is right there with me. For in my inner being I delight in God's law; but I see another law at work in the members of my body, waging war against the law of my mind and making me a prisoner of the law of sin at work within my members. What a wretched man I am! Who will rescue me from this body of death? Thanks be to God— through Jesus Christ our Lord!

So then, I myself in my mind am a slave to God's law, but in the sinful nature a slave to the law of sin.

Therefore, there is now no condemnation for those who are in Christ Jesus, because through Christ Jesus the law of the Spirit of life set me free from the law of sin and death. For what the law was powerless to do in that it was weakened by the sinful nature, God did by sending his own Son in the likeness of sinful man to be a sin offering. And so he condemned sin in sinful man, in order that the righteous requirements of the law might be fully met in us, who do not live according to the sinful nature but according to the Spirit. (Rom. 7:14–8:4)

The Apostle Peter wrote, "Dear friends, I urge you, as aliens and strangers in the world, to abstain from sinful desires, which war against your soul" (1 Pet. 2:11).

The Book of James says, "When tempted, no one should say, 'God is tempting me.' For God cannot be tempted by evil, nor does he tempt anyone; but each one is tempted when, by his own evil desire, he is dragged away and enticed. Then, after desire has conceived, it gives birth to sin; and sin, when it is full-grown, gives birth to death" (James 1:13–15).

These passages show that all human beings are prone to sinful desires, temptations, and lusts. Your mate is no exception. You can provide spiritual support by refusing to deny your human frailties, acknowledging these inner battles, and joining together to pray for each other to have victory in the areas where you each are most vulnerable.

Practice

⧗ Identify a battle in your own life that has the characteristics identified in the passages of Scripture above. This would be something you inwardly desire even though you know it is wrong. Perhaps it is something the Holy Spirit has convicted you of, yet you are enticed by it so that—if allowed to prevail—it would give birth to sin.

⧗ Every person has areas of particular weakness in which they struggle. These are categorized in Galatians 5:17–21. Read this passage on your own. Refer to the following list, where some of the phrases are defined, and choose a category where you have an inner struggle.

You might want to start with something that is not a major battle. Today you are learning to enter into these kinds of spiritual battles on each other's behalf. Once you learn to do so and gain each other's trust to deal with potentially shameful issues, you can go on to share more difficult battles.

Some of the things that fall into the category of inner battles include:

- sexual temptation

- gluttony or other obsession with eating

- addictions such as alcohol, nicotine, drugs, gambling

- out-of-control spending

- impure thoughts

- prejudice

- self-righteousness

- arrogance

- pride

- hatred

- greed

- jealousy

- envy

- a tendency to gossip or backbite

- a judgmental or condemning spirit

- idolatry—putting anything above your devotion to God

- superstition or occultic practices

- discord with others

- outbursts of anger or uncontrollable rage

- selfish ambition

- dissension

- bitterness

- resentment

- inappropriate speech

- unforgiveness

- covetousness

⌛ Take turns listening to each other as you describe one inner battle for which you would like to have your mate as a spiritual ally. List your inner battles here.

Husband: _____

_____

Wife: _____

_____

⌛ Are you willing to commit yourself to enter this spiritual battle in prayer on your mate's behalf? (This means that you will take on this issue as a matter of prayer, consideration, and reflection until the Lord gives victory or gives your mate closure regarding this struggle. This will also involve listening to your spouse so that you can pray with insight on his or her behalf as long as the struggle continues.) Husband: _____ Wife: _____

⌛ The key to overcoming our inner battles is not to put each other "under the law" by focusing on the problem and demanding that the inner cravings or tendencies stop, but rather to focus on the solution: Jesus Christ and the grace of God, which will give your mate the power and guidance to win this inner battle. If you are in the habit of nagging each other about anything related to this inner struggle, make a commitment to turn every temptation to nag into a commitment to "nag" God on your mate's behalf in prayer about this inner battle.

You can help each other overcome the flesh by understanding and meditating on God's Word related to such struggles. The following are passages of Scripture that address such issues. You can help each other by turning what you learn in these verses into prayers on each other's behalf. As you pray for each other with regard to these stated inner struggles, also study the following passages to grow in your understanding of how God sets us free from bondage within. If time is short, you don't have to read these now. You can use them for an extended study or for future reference.

Romans 6:12–14   Romans 7:9–8:8   Romans 13:12–14   Galatians 5:16–6:5

Ephesians 2:1–10   Colossians 3:1–19   1 Timothy 6:9–12   2 Timothy 2:22

James 1:19–22   James 4:1–17   1 Peter 4:1–8   2 Peter 1:1–12

Most of these passages deal with inner battles by changing something in the inner being: changing an attitude, focusing on the promises of God, focusing on the grace of God. Try to help each other by becoming familiar with these passages and by making the positive inner changes the Bible says to make. Remember, only as Christians walk by the power of the Holy Spirit are they able to overcome the sinful nature. Inner battles are fought and won in the mind as it is renewed by the Word of God. They are won in the realm of your will when you bring your will in line with God's will. The power comes from the Holy Spirit as you engage your faith to believe the promises God has given you. You can continually pray that your mate will think in accordance with God's Word and choose to agree with God.

Promises

God's Promise to You
"So I say, live by the Spirit, and you will not gratify the desires of the sinful nature" (Gal. 5:16).

Your Promise to Each Other
To become spiritual allies with regard to each other's inner battles, praying instead of nagging, and not condemning.

Prayer

Our Father in heaven,

Please help us understand how to walk by the power of your Holy Spirit. As we confide in each other regarding our inner spiritual battles, please show us how to pray for each other. Help us not to condemn each other, but instead to help each other set our minds, hearts, and attitudes in line with your will. Please renew our minds with your truth, which can free us from the desires of our sinful nature. Lord, please help us be true spiritual allies even when the battles we each face are within. In Jesus' name. Amen!

WEEK SIX

Come Together to Accomplish God's Purpose in Home and Family

Introduction

God has a set purpose for your home and family. He has a purpose for each of you as a bridge between generations, in your marriage, in relationship to your children, and in the way your home operates. When you focus on God's overall purpose for your home and family and realize that God is working with you to fulfill his purpose, you find a greater sense of purpose, greater power from on high to draw on, and a greater anticipation of how good life can be. Don't let past failures or family problems be the focus of your life. Instead, focus on God's purpose for you and your family. Let that dictate the direction of your future family life.

Man to Man

with Bill McCartney

Success has many definitions. I like this one: Success comes when those who know you the best love you the most. All of our shortcomings are clear to those at home. Likewise are our redeeming qualities. Jesus would have us team up with our wives and put it all on the table at home. It doesn't matter how great people "out there" think you are if you can't get along with and minister to the people in your family the way God wants you to. That's what I realized late in life. But it's never too late to go home.

Some time ago, a coaching colleague of mine asked for a meeting. I had been out of coaching three years. Jon, age thirty-three, expressed frustration trying to balance the needs at home with the demands of major college football. I offered this advice. "In the time I've had away from coaching, I have learned plenty. I see it so much more clearly than I could in the midst of the rigors of pressing game plans. Jon, go home! When you get to the driveway, collect yourself. Pray for perspective. Walk through those doors with a determination to love and serve. Forget about fatigue. Fight through self-pity. Be the man your wife and children desire and deserve." I believe this advice can help every married man, regardless of his occupation. When you go home, go home to love and open your heart to your family.

Being open with your family isn't easy. But adversity can draw us closer to those we love most. As we are transparent, vulnerable, and exposed before the Lord together, the healing can begin in our families. When we come united before the Lord, he knits our hearts together. He teaches us to love and receive love. If it's not happening at home, whatever else you're doing really doesn't matter.

Woman to Woman

with Lyndi McCartney

While traveling through airports across this nation, I enjoy people watching. It's my unscientific observation that people are not very nice to each other. Seems they often bump into circumstances while traveling that cause the fruit of the Spirit to fall off their trees. In addition to traveling through airports, I have the opportunity to visit many churches, and what a contrast I see. Smiles and warmth, hugs and prayers. While there may be occasional children that get on their parents' nerves from time to time, churches are great places to regenerate those frayed nerves and observe people caring for one another.

Our homes are the foundations of the churches, but so many of our homes have turned into fractured battlefields where crimes of the heart are committed against our loved ones. It's time for us to reflect and—if need be—repent. It's time to turn from our own ways and turn toward God. Jesus can heal our fractured homes. Jesus can clear away the battlefields and replace them with fields ready to harvest. Jesus can end the crimes and heal the wounds, but we have to turn to him for these changes to begin.

This week's exercises can help the healing begin or continue—for husband and wife, for parents and children. These are the very steps we took to begin the healing and return wholeness in God to our family. It's not just a week's study; it's also a new life to live daily. My husband asked me during a very fragile time in our healing process to make a list for him of the ways I feel loved by him. It was a time when negativity was the norm for me. What a huge difference it made to tell him how I felt loved by him. My list reinforced the good he did; it brought back the good he used to do and incorporated a few new things. My husband took the positives and committed them to prayer daily. It made such a difference in our life. Ask your husband and children how you make them feel loved. Their answers will give you great insight into their needs as individuals.

Purpose

- To recognize patterns of life that are passed from generation to generation

- To identify sinful patterns that have been passed down to your family

- To break the pattern of sin in this generation and pass down a godly heritage

- To begin to restore the ruins of many generations

Premise

The Bible shows us that sinful and destructive patterns of life are passed down from generation to generation unless there is godly intervention. When Moses recounted God's Ten Commandments to the people of Israel, he said, "You shall not make for yourself an idol in the form of anything in heaven above or on the earth beneath or in the waters below. You shall not bow down to them or worship them; for I, the LORD your God, am a jealous God, punishing the children for the sin of the fathers to the third and fourth generation of those who hate me, but showing love to a thousand generations of those who love me and keep my commandments" (Exod. 20:4–6).

There are numerous examples of both good and bad, godly and sinful patterns influencing the succeeding generations in family lines. Abram/Abraham's deception, saying that his wife was his sister, was repeated by his son, Isaac. Jacob cheated his brother out of his birthright by creating an elaborate deception to trick his father. In turn, Jacob was cheated repeatedly by his father-in-law, and his own sons created an elaborate deception to trick him into believing that his son Joseph had been killed when he had not. King David began his foray into sin on the roof of the palace where he saw Bathsheba bathing next door. He used his power to have illicit sex that led to murder. This became a national incident. Many years later, King David's son Amnon used his power to have illicit sex with David's daughter Tamar. David's son Absalom then murdered Amnon and later rebelled against his father. Then he went up on the roof of the palace and had sex with his father's concubines in the sight of all of Israel. Throughout Scripture the repetitive nature of sin throughout generations is conclusive—even in families devoted to God.

We are also told that God has given us a way to break the pattern of sin and the suffering it brings to succeeding generations. We can change our lives in this generation in a way that will allow us to pass down a godly heritage and the fruit of righteousness to our children and our children's children. When Mary, while pregnant with Jesus, came to her cousin Elizabeth, she announced this change. She said, "For the Mighty One has done great things for me—holy is his name. His mercy extends to those who fear him, from generation to generation" (Luke 1:49–50). In Jesus Christ we have the promise that we are not doomed simply to live in the ongoing consequences of the sins of past generations. Rather, those who follow God can pass on God's mercy from generation to generation.

We see a beautiful example of the pattern of God's mercy being passed on to succeeding generations in the life of Timothy. His father was a Greek unbeliever, but even with only one Christian parent Timothy received and carried on a godly heritage. Paul wrote to Timothy, "I have been reminded of your sincere faith, which first lived in your grandmother Lois and in your mother Eunice and, I am persuaded, now lives in you also" (2 Tim. 1:5). If this is the case with a young man who only had one believing parent, imagine the potential godly legacy that can be passed on by a husband and wife sold out to God together. And even if you do not have children, you can pass on a godly heritage to the young people in your extended family who do not have the influence of godly parents. You can also pass on a godly heritage to those in the younger generation who you can influence in your church (perhaps teaching Sunday School or working in the youth ministry), in your workplace, and in the larger community.

In addition to breaking the sinful pattern, we can begin to restore the ruins of many generations. This is the heritage God has given to all his children, and you can impart it to your children if you work together to do so. We see this in the prophecy of Isaiah 61. This passage foreshadowed the ministry of the Messiah. Jesus said he fulfilled the first three verses when he preached in the synagogue in Nazareth. However, further down we see these promises:

> They will be called oaks of righteousness,
>> a planting of the LORD
>> for the display of his splendor.
> They will rebuild the ancient ruins
>> and restore the places long devastated;
> they will renew the ruined cities
>> that have been devastated for generations. (Isa. 61:3b–4)

> For I, the LORD, love justice;
>> I hate robbery and iniquity.
> In my faithfulness I will reward them
>> and make an everlasting covenant with them. (Isa. 61:8)

This covenant refers to the New Covenant Jesus announced at the Last Supper when he "took the cup, saying, 'This cup is the new covenant in my blood, which is poured out for you'" (Luke 22:20). This is also explained in Hebrews 9:15: "Christ is the mediator of a new covenant, that those who are called may receive the promised eternal inheritance—now that he has died as a ransom to set them free from the sins committed under the first covenant."

The prophecy in Isaiah 61:9 continues with an application for future generations:

> Their descendants will be known among the nations
>> and their offspring among the peoples.
> All who see them will acknowledge
>> that they are a people the LORD has blessed.

All those who have entered into the New Covenant with the Lord through the blood of Jesus can align their lives with God's will by determining to "rebuild the ancient ruins and restore the places long devastated" and to renew the places that "have been devastated for generations."

Practice

⏳ If time is short, be careful not to spend too much time discussing each element. Focus on identifying the key item or items you want to pray about. You can come back and discuss these issues further at another time.

1. Identify the patterns of sin that are apparent in your family line on both sides. Look for things like dishonesty, divorce, any kind of immoral sexual activity, alcoholism, drug addiction, compulsions, criminal behavior, greed, child abuse, violence—whatever patterns you see. You may choose to list physical conditions or predispositions, such as mental illness or obesity, that may or may not be related to behavior that falls into areas of sin. You don't have to know if something is passed down genetically or spiritually to bring it before the Lord and seek his help in breaking destructive patterns. List the patterns you see here.

    Husband   Wife

    _____   _____
    _____   _____
    _____   _____
    _____   _____

2. Identify and discuss how either of you have continued in or struggled against sinful patterns that are apparent in past generations of your family lineage.

3. Identify any symptoms or patterns of sin you already see in your children or the next generation of your family that follow your family's past history.

    Husband   Wife

    _____   _____
    _____   _____
    _____   _____
    _____   _____

4. Determine to live your life and raise your children according to the truths of the New Covenant. This means that you can acknowledge your own sins if you are willing to confess, repent, receive forgiveness for them, and forsake these sinful ways by the power of the Holy Spirit. You can accept your responsibility as a Christian to confront sin honestly when you see it in others—particularly those in your family—and provide godly correction for your children. Many parents, perhaps King David included, feel disqualified to correct sins in their children if they have committed those sins themselves. You must not allow that to happen! Even if you have sinned, determine to make that wrong a learning experience for your children. Given the truth of God's forgiveness, you can turn your own painful past into examples to teach your children the consequences of sin and God's power to free us from bondage.

5. Repent of the sins you see in your life that repeat patterns from your family. Choose to renounce these patterns and any tendency to excuse sinful behavior because it "runs in our family."

6. Agree to pray together with regard to these patterns (as will be modeled for you in today's prayer). Also add these to the list of inner spiritual battles you will cover in prayer for your mate. Pray for each other about these patterns and take all necessary action so they will not be passed down to your children.

Promises

God's Promise to You
"But from everlasting to everlasting the LORD's love is with those who fear him, and his righteousness with their children's children—with those who keep his covenant and remember to obey his precepts" (Ps. 103:17–18).

Your Promise to Each Other
To agree together to pass on a godly heritage to the next generation in the fear of the Lord.

Prayer

Use this prayer as an outline that you can expand with the details of your family history and the particular needs you see in your children and grandchildren.

Our Father in heaven,

Lord you know all the sins of the past generations of our family and how these sins have brought pain and sorrow to many. We bring before you the patterns of sin—and perhaps sickness—that have been repeated in our family. (Pray out the list you made earlier.) In Jesus' name, we ask you to break these destructive patterns in our family. We claim the forgiveness and restoration you intended when you put the New Covenant into effect by the blood of Jesus. Lord we each confess our sins that follow in the patterns we now see in our family lines. (Take turns confessing any sins or struggles with sinful patterns from your family line that you listed earlier.) Thank you for sending the blood of Jesus that cleanses us from all sin. Lord, we also choose to forgive the sins that have been committed against us by family members. Please bring these to mind so we can forgive them one by one, so the sins of others will not hold us in bondage.

Lord, we pray for our children and grandchildren—born and as yet unborn. Please help us to pass on a godly heritage to them. Please give us the confidence in your forgiveness and your Word to confront and correct sins in their lives, even if we have sinned in the same ways ourselves. Please free us entirely from such sins so that we are not impaired in our ability to correct our children. We pray for particular patterns of sin and sickness that we can already see beginning in the next generation. (List these here.) Lord, we pray you free them. In Jesus' name. Amen!

Day Two
Make Your Marriage What God Intended It to Be

Purpose

- To remind yourselves of God's purposes for your marriage

- To return to your first love by bringing your sexual relationship back to what God intended

- To see that you are loving each other according to God's definition of love

Premise

Even though we can only touch on what it means to fulfill God's purposes in your marriage in this session, we dare not skip this vital aspect of your lives. Your marriage has deep spiritual significance. Ephesians 5:31–32 links the marital union to the mysterious union of Jesus Christ with the church. This suggests that Christian marriage can be a living example of the Lord's relationship with his bride. Your marriage has a profound influence on your children. One of the best things you can do to help your children feel loved and secure is to openly display true love for each other in your home. Your marriage can also provide a powerful witness to the people who know you or are acquainted with you. When you love each other as God designed you to, those around you will see a visible display of the kind of love relationship God wants to have with them.

While we don't have time to explore all the passages of Scripture that relate marriage to a picture of God's love for his people, here are a few that you can consider on your own: the Book of Hosea, Song of Solomon, Isaiah 54, and Revelation 19:7–9.

The sexual union between husband and wife is sacred. Scripture reveals that the intimate union of husband and wife is representative of Christ and his bride. Ephesians 5:31–33 says, "'For this reason a man will leave his father and mother and be united to his wife, and the two will become one flesh.' This is a profound mystery—but I am talking about Christ and the church. However, each one of you also must love his wife as he loves himself, and the wife must respect her husband." Is it any wonder that Satan seems to work overtime to sully or destroy this sacred aspect of marriage?

Scripture makes it clear that maintaining a loving, intimate relationship is part of a healthy Christian marriage. It says, "The husband should fulfill his marital duty to his wife, and likewise the wife to her husband. The wife's body does not belong to her alone but also to her husband. In the same way, the husband's body does not belong to him alone but also to his wife. Do not deprive each other except by mutual consent and for a time, so that you may devote yourselves to prayer. Then come together again so that Satan will not tempt you because of your lack of self-control" (1 Cor. 7:3–5).

God intended man and woman to be "naked and unashamed" as it says in Genesis 2:25. However, after being deceived by the serpent in the garden, Adam and Eve began to hide from each other and to blame each other. Just as Satan set out to destroy the sacred sexual union between Adam and Eve, he also tries to undermine and destroy the intimate union between every husband and wife. Therefore, expect to fight some spiritual battles with regard to your sexual union. Don't shy away. God wants you to be blessed in your sexual union.

The blessing of intimate love should be something all Christian couples pursue until they receive the love and blessings God intended in this area of their lives. God can forgive and redeem any sexual sin done by or against either of you. God can restore what he originally intended for your relationship and help you enjoy the blessings of sexual union that mirror the love Christ has for his bride.

The love you express to each other intimately will flow out of the quality of love you have for each other in every other area of your lives. Today you can take a fresh look at how well you are loving each other and make changes so that the love you express toward each other, intimately and in all areas of life, is what God intended.

Practice

✠ Start by taking a refresher course in love by God's definition. Read 1 Corinthians 13:1–3 as quoted here. Then answer the questions.

> If I speak in the tongues of men and of angels, but have not love, I am only a resounding gong or a clanging cymbal. If I have the gift of prophecy and can fathom all mysteries and all knowledge, and if I have a faith that can move mountains, but have not love, I am nothing. If I give all I possess to the poor and surrender my body to the flames, but have not love, I gain nothing.

What religious acts of devotion and spiritual gifts are mentioned in these verses? _____

_____

According to this passage of Scripture, what do any of these spiritual "successes" accomplish if they are done without love? _____

_____

✠ Read 1 Corinthians 13:4–8a as quoted here.

> Love is patient, love is kind. It does not envy, it does not boast, it is not proud. It is not rude, it is not self-seeking, it is not easily angered, it keeps no record of wrongs. Love does not delight in evil but rejoices with the truth. It always protects, always trusts, always hopes, always perseveres. Love never fails.

The chart given below allows you to break down the definition of love into specific attitudes and actions. Paraphrase as necessary. For example, the verse says, "it keeps no record of wrongs." List this under the heading "Love does not . . ." You might complete the statement with: "keep a record of wrongs." You may have only one item in some columns and several in others.

Love is . . . Love is not . . . Love does not . . . Love always . . . Love . . . Love never . . .

———	———	———	———	———	———
———	———	———	———	———	———
———	———	———	———	———	———
———	———	———	———	———	———
———	———	———	———	———	———
———	———	———	———	———	———

⧗ According to this definition of love, consider specific ways you need to change in order to truly love your mate. List any you can think of for yourself here.

Husband	Wife
———————	———————
———————	———————
———————	———————

Galatians 5:13–15 says, "You, my brothers, were called to be free. But do not use your freedom to indulge the sinful nature; rather, serve one another in love. The entire law is summed up in a single command: 'Love your neighbor as yourself.' If you keep on biting and devouring each other, watch out or you will be destroyed by each other." All Christians need to be careful not to do anything that is unloving, selfish, or destructive to their mates—especially in the area of sex. This includes making sure you are expressing love and unselfishness in the way you relate to each other intimately.

Following is a two-column list. On the left are Scripture references for passages related to marriage. On the right are the blessings and purposes marriage was meant to accomplish mentioned in the passages. Look up the Scripture passages and draw a line between each reference and the description of the blessing or purpose of marriage. Let this set your mind to remember the overall purpose of marriage rather than focus only on the "leaky" spots that need to be fixed.

⧗ If time is short, read and think about the list at right. You can go back later to check the Scripture references that substantiate the statements.

Genesis 2:18	In marriage, God intended us to be naked without shame.
Genesis 2:20–22	God intended marriage to be a relationship where wives experience the kind of love they long for—the kind of love Christ has for his church.
Genesis 2:24	God created marriage to be a relationship in which a man would receive the kind of respect he longs for and needs.
Genesis 2:25	God made marriage so we wouldn't have to be alone.
Ephesians 5:25	Marriage was created as a mysterious revelation of the love Jesus Christ has for his church, for all the world to see.
Ephesians 5:31	God created the sexual union as a blessed way to become one flesh.
Ephesians 5:33	God made marriage to provide needed help and companionship.

⧖ Take some time today to practice directing your thoughts to the grand purposes God had in mind when he brought the two of you together. Use these passages of Scripture as the basis for meditating on what God intends to do in and through your marriage. Feel free to share your thoughts on this topic with each other as they arise.

⧖ Plan time this week to be together intimately. Before you do, think of the kind of love you had for each other when you were first married and do some of the things you used to do to bless each other. Focus on giving rather than trying to get your needs met. Try to outdo each other in showing love.

Think about how generous you are in your intimate relationship with your mate. Make a decision to demonstrate your love by being a generous lover. You'll both benefit.

Promises

God's Promise to You
"Love never fails!" (1 Cor. 13:8a).

Your Promise to Each Other
To intentionally love each other as God intended.

Prayer

Our Father in heaven,

Thank you for creating the sexual relationship in which we become one flesh as husband and wife. This is a profound mystery! To think that this represents your love for the church is awesome. And yet there have been times that our relationship has fallen from the good one you intended it to be. Lord, please forgive us for any times we used or hurt each other in our intimate relationship. Please forgive and free us from any unholy sexual practices that mar and undermine the relationship you ordained for us. Please help us bless each other sexually and through the love we show each other in every way. In Jesus' name. Amen!

Day Three
Set Godly Goals for Your Family with Binocular Vision

Purpose

- To consider specific things God would have you do to accomplish his purposes for your family

- To look at your family's future, drawing from each unique perspective for the overall good of your family

- To identify many worthy goals that are in keeping with the family-related commands and principles found in the Bible

- To commit yourselves to some specific goals that fulfill God's commands and biblical principles related to family life

Premise

God has taken hold of each person for a reason. We each have a mission in life that relates to whether we are married and have children. When you marry and if you have children, your mission in life will necessarily grow to include conducting family life in keeping with God's commands. As you fulfill your responsibilities as a marriage partner and parent, you can be confident you are fulfilling God's plan for your life.

The Apostle Paul showed his sense of mission when he wrote, "Not that I have already obtained all this, or have already been made perfect, but I press on to take hold of that for which Christ Jesus took hold of me. Brothers, I do not consider myself yet to have taken hold of it. But one thing I do: Forgetting what is behind and straining toward what is ahead, I press on toward the goal to win the prize for which God has called me heavenward in Christ Jesus" (Phil. 3:12–14). Today you will think about what goals are worthy of your commitment as you seek to fulfill God's purpose for your lives.

When you sit down together to consider the future of your family and what goals you want to set, you each bring different perspectives, a differing sense of what is most important. You may each look at particular children and have a different understanding of them. You may find that you look at the same situation and have differing attitudes, approaches, and ideas about how to accomplish a purpose you both agree on.

Approaching goal setting for your family together can be likened to being able to see farther and better through binoculars. God made men and women different, with the ability to come together in family life and bring unique perspectives. This can be an advantage if you learn to combine your perspectives instead of competing with each other. One's sensitivity and awareness of motives can work together with the other's practical approach. As you approach your discussions and decisions today try to benefit from each other's perspective.

Practice

⧗ Each of the following Scripture references can give you insight into something you might want to incorporate into a goal for your family. Some of these verses were directed to a particular person or group but still hold an inference you can use to create a worthy goal for your family. Look up the references on the left in your Bible. Then have your partner read the comment at right that rephrases the verses into a possible goal you may want to adapt or adopt for your family.

⧗ We've given you more than you can possibly do in thirty minutes. We suggest you choose a few of these that are most meaningful to you and complete the application to your family now. You may choose to read the remaining verses now and make the applications as they come to mind or come back to them later.

After reading each, discuss and decide on a *specific* application you can make as a goal for your family. This is where you will need to bring the perspectives of husband and wife together in binocular vision. Some examples are provided to get you started.

Scripture Reference	Personal Application to Turn into a Godly Goal

Proverbs 1:8   As parents, to give our children instruction and personally teach them what they should know.

Example of a family goal from this verse: To teach our children right from wrong, read them the gospel, and instruct them as to how they can come to know Jesus Christ as their personal Lord and Savior.

1 Peter 4:9   To offer each other hospitality at home without grumbling.

Example of a family goal from this verse: To practice saying please, thank you, and I'm sorry whenever appropriate. To take action to serve each other in practical ways. To practice being thoughtful of each other.

2 Corinthians 12:14b   To manage our finances well enough to be able to save up for our children's future financial needs.

Example of a personalized family goal from this verse: To begin saving a set amount of money each month toward each child's college fund.

John 15:12–13   To love each other in ways that demonstrate self-sacrifice.

_____

_____

1 Peter 4:8   When sins are revealed—even a multitude of sins—to love each other deeply enough, keep loving and forgiving.

_____

_____

Ephesians 4:31   To get rid of all bitterness, rage, anger, brawling, slander, and every form of malice.

_____

_____

Ephesians 4:32   To practice being kind and compassionate to one another, forgiving each other, just as in Christ, God forgave us.

_____

_____

_____

Deuteronomy 4:9   To be careful and watch ourselves closely so that we don't forget the things we have seen God do or let them slip from our hearts as long as we live. To teach these things to our children.

_____

_____

_____

Deuteronomy 4:10   To assemble together with God's people (in church) to hear God's Word. To teach our children to revere the Lord.

_____

_____

_____

Deuteronomy 4:13   To teach our children the Ten Commandments.

_____

_____

Deuteronomy 6:5–7   To love the Lord our God with all our heart and with all our soul and with all our strength. To keep God's commandments on our own hearts so that we can impress them on our children.

_____

_____

_____

Deuteronomy 6:7–9   To make God's Word a part of everyday home life: talking about it when we sit at home and when we go through the course of our day, when we lie down and when we get up. To make God's Word a visible presence in our home.

_____

_____

_____

Mark 10:14   To let our children come to Jesus; to do nothing that hinders them from coming into his kingdom.

_____

_____

Luke 1:17   As a father, to turn my heart to my children in an effort to make them prepared for the Lord.

_____

_____

Acts 2:38   To encourage our children to do what we have already done, to repent and be baptized in the name of Jesus Christ for the forgiveness of our sins. To encourage them to receive the gift of the Holy Spirit.

_____

_____

Acts 21:5   To be in the practice of dealing with important life events by kneeling down together to pray as a family.

_____

_____

Ephesians 6:4 and   To bring up our children in the training and instruction
1 Timothy 5:10   of the Lord, but not to exasperate them.

_____

_____

Colossians 3:21   To be sensitive about what could embitter or discourage our children. To live so as to encourage them in the Lord.

_____

_____

1 Thessalonians 2:11–12   To encourage and comfort our children, urging them to live lives worthy of God, who calls them into his kingdom.

_____

_____

1 Timothy 3:4 and
1 Timothy 5:14   To manage our family well so our children are obedient and learn to show proper respect and so the enemy has no opportunity for slander.

_____

_____

Titus 1:6   To raise our children to believe in the Lord and not be wild and disobedient.

_____

_____

Matthew 15:4–6   To help take care of our aging parents when they need help.

_____

_____

List any other godly goals you want to make for your family here. _____

_____

_____

⧗ Check any of the goals above that you agree to pursue together for your family. List any specific action you can take today to start working together toward these goals.

_____

_____

Promises

God's Promise to You
"'For I know the plans I have for you,' declares the LORD, 'plans to prosper you and not to harm you, plans to give you hope and a future. Then you will call upon me and come and pray to me, and I will listen to you. You will seek me and find me when you seek me with all your heart'" (Jer. 29:11–13).

Your Promise to Each Other
To set goals together that will help you live out God's purposes for your family in practical and intentional ways.

Prayer

Our Father in heaven,

You have given us many practical instructions as to how we are to conduct ourselves in family life. In our hearts we want to fulfill your purpose for our family. Please help us to go beyond hoping our family life will be what you want it to be. Help us make commitments, set goals, and encourage each other to obey your instructions in practical ways. Lord, you know the goals we have chosen in today's exercise. Please help us to follow through, to do what we have set ourselves to do. Please give us the power of your Holy Spirit to accomplish your purposes in our family life. In Jesus' name. Amen!

Day Four
Discover and Use Family Resources
Available through Your Church

Purpose

- To consider the ways in which your church could help your family accomplish God's purposes for you

- To discover what family-related resources are available through your local church

- To get involved with your church in ways that can help your family accomplish God's purposes for you

Premise

Regardless of the denomination, every church aims to help the families in its congregation. Most churches have resources that will help you understand the Bible's teachings related to roles, responsibilities, blessings, and relationships within the family. Your church may have classes to help you develop skills that will equip you to better fulfill your God-given responsibilities and become a blessing to the other members of your family. Your church has children's programs that can help you fulfill your responsibility to make sure your children learn God's Word and hear the gospel. Your church may also have marriage classes, retreats, men's ministry, women's ministry, target groups such as "Mothers of Pre-Schoolers," or small groups that deal with overcoming some sin or problem that can harm your family. Your pastor or pastoral staff can also be a source of godly counsel when you face times of crisis or particular problems.

God has provided the local church as the place to grow in our faith and learn how to live with each other in accordance with God's Word. However, many Christians don't make the most of what God has provided. You may be so busy that you only go to church on Sundays and have never taken the time to explore the other resources available. You may or may not have familiarized yourself with what your church provides, but that is what you will focus on today as a way of helping yourselves fulfill God's purpose for your family.

Practice

⧖ Do one or more of the following to identify resources available to you. If time is short, you may want to decide which one of you will do what part of the research and follow through at a later time.

- Make a list of all the ministries you are aware of within your church that could help your family. Don't forget your church library, tape lending library, or tapes of past sermons that provide resources you can use on your own.

- Refer to past church bulletins, newsletters, or other materials that you may not have looked at carefully before. Note all the programs that could be of help to any member of your family.

- Call your church office and ask someone to send you a comprehensive schedule of classes or a brochure outlining the programs and materials available that could be of help to your family.

⧖ List each member of your family on the next page. Under each name, list the programs, resources, special events, or other services provided by your church that could help that person grow in the ways of the Lord. (For the purpose of today's exercise choose only those things that can help your family members. Next week you will consider how you can get involved in your church to help others.) We've given some basic examples. You can elaborate with the detailed information you find in researching your own church.

Husband	Wife	Child #1	Child #2	Child #3	Child #4
PK Groups	Women's Bible Study	Youth Group	Children's Choir	Children's Choir	Nursery
Marriage Class	Marriage Class	Missions Trip with Sr. High	Vacation Bible School	Vacation Bible School	Mommy and Me exercise
Couples Retreat	Couples Retreat	Youth Bible Study			
	Mommy and Me exercise	Class on how to get along with parents			
Bible Study on Ephesians	Bible Study on Ephesians	Counseling			
Books on marriage and parenting	Books on marriage and parenting	Prayer support			

Fill in the chart below based on your family. (Continue to complete this chart as you gain information.)

Husband	Wife	Child #1	Child #2	Child #3	Child #4

⧗ It may take you some time to gather information about all the resources available through your church. If you can't find it immediately, make the commitment to gather the material and go over it together before a specific day next week, which you will record here.

We will commit ourselves to continue gathering information about the resources available to help our family. We will meet again to discuss this by next _____, the _____ day of _____, _____.

Signature: _____

Signature: _____

When you resume your discussion of these resources, decide which ones you need the most and when you will participate. List that information here.

The programs and resources our church provides that we will use to help our family include.

Name of Program or Resource	Who It's For	Date and Time
_____	_____	_____
_____	_____	_____
_____	_____	_____
_____	_____	_____
_____	_____	_____
_____	_____	_____

Promises

God's Promise to You
"If you accept my words and store up my commands within you, turning your ear to wisdom and applying your heart to understanding, and if you call out for insight and cry aloud for understanding, and if you look for it as for silver and search for it as for hidden treasure, then you will understand the fear of the LORD and find the knowledge of God" (Prov. 2:1–5).

Your Promise to Each Other
To use resources in your church to help your family grow.

Prayer

Our Father in heaven,

Thank you for the resources you have given us in our local church. Lord we pray your blessing on our pastor and all those who minister to us in this body. Please help us to use these resources to help each member of our family grow and fulfill your purpose. In Jesus' name. Amen!

Day Five
Correct Past Neglect of Family Relationships and Responsibilities

Purpose

- To identify where you have each neglected family relationships and responsibilities

- To apologize as necessary and ask forgiveness for what your lapse has caused in the lives of the other members of your family

- To take action to correct your past neglect in some specific way

Premise

In this day and age, most people are too busy. Most tend to be too busy to fully enjoy and satisfy the needs for relationship within their immediate family. Many are torn in several different directions; they continually sense they are failing to fulfill the most important responsibilities in their lives—the responsibilities within their own home and family. We would be remiss not to address this and give you the opportunity to take at least small steps toward correcting any neglect in your family life.

Today's exercises will not go too deep in exploring particular family responsibilities. What we will do is give you the opportunity to discuss things the Holy Spirit may have already brought to mind as you have spent the past four days thinking about God's mission and purpose for your family.

In the past four days, you may have felt a twinge of true guilt—the conviction of the Holy Spirit—over some area where you know you are falling short of what God would have you do within your family. God has a remedy for such guilt and uses the conviction of the Holy Spirit to get you to change your life to come into line with God's will so you can benefit from his blessings.

This is *not* a time for you to get out your list of how you think your mate is falling short in his or her family relationships and responsibilities. This is a time for you to share with each other areas where you are being convicted by the Holy Spirit, areas where *you* need to change for the good of your family. This will not be a once-and-for-all deal. God has the rest of your lives to change you in many ways that will benefit your family and help you fulfill God's purposes. As you help each other through this process, you will train yourselves to continue helping each other change to benefit your family throughout life.

Practice

⧗ Several of the following items could turn into lengthy discussions. Stay focused for the purpose of today's exercise. You can come back to these areas later and continue your discussions, as well as continue in prayer about these issues.

⧗ 1. Spend a few moments in prayer together asking the Holy Spirit to convict your hearts of specific areas where you have neglected your family relationships and responsibilities.

⧗ 2. Share with each other one or two things that you sense are areas where you need correction with regard to your family relationships and responsibilities. Complete this statement: The area I need to correct in order to better fulfill my family relationships and responsibilities is . . .

⧗ 3. Identify to each other what you would need to do to change this area—even if you don't see any way you can correct it right now. For example, you may know that you need to spend more time with your children, but the demands of work have you stretched to your limits. You may not be able to afford to cut back on your hours or change jobs right now. Yet you may feel convicted about this regularly. Go ahead and identify what you need to do—even though you are not free to do so given current circumstances. Complete this statement: In order to correct this I would . . .

⧗ 4. Pray together and ask God to show you what you can do to make these corrections. If there are circumstances outside of your control, ask God to change them or give you the courage to change the circumstances within your control.

⧗ 5. Identify what you can do *today* to make a positive change—even a small change. Then do it! Complete this statement: Today I can correct my neglect of my family by . . .

Promises

God's Promise to You

"Therefore, O house of Israel, I will judge you, each one according to his ways, declares the Sovereign LORD. Repent! Turn away from all your offenses; then sin will not be your downfall" (Ezek. 18:30).

Your Promise to Each Other

To examine your own life in light of your God-given family responsibilities and seek to change where change is necessary.

Prayer

Our Father in heaven,

We are aware of how we fall short of fulfilling our family responsibilities as you would have us. We need your help. We need your wisdom. We need courage to make the choices that will allow us to be available for our family as we are needed. Lord, we ask you to continue to speak to us about areas where we have fallen short of your best in loving and meeting the needs of those in our family. Please give us hope to know that you can change us and our relationships. Lord, please help both of us see our errors, confess our sins and shortcomings, and look to you to change. Lord, please make our family all that you created it to be. In Jesus' name. Amen!

WEEK SEVEN

Come Together to Fulfill God's
Purpose in Your Local Church

Introduction

God called those who would follow Jesus into the local church. Within the church, God established standards for the communication of true doctrine, for relationships that will equip all members to become fully functioning in their various gifts and abilities so that they can contribute to the building up of the body of Christ. He also established a procedure for correction and discipline to maintain purity and deal with error or sin in the lives of his people. It is in the context of church relationships that we are challenged to love each other, forgive each other, encourage each other, and—if necessary—restore each other.

Scripturally, church participation is not optional. We are to be committed to a fellowship of believers and submitted to the leadership of the congregation. The first church assembled after the ascension of Jesus, and "they devoted themselves to the apostles' teaching and to the fellowship, to the breaking of bread and to prayer" (Acts 2:42). So, too, we are to assemble together to receive biblical instruction, to participate in fellowship with other believers, to build relationships with each other, and to pray together.

In fact, the closer we draw to the return of Jesus Christ, the more diligent we should be in our church participation. This is clearly stated in Hebrews 10:25, "Let us not give up meeting together, as some are in the habit of doing, but let us encourage one another—and all the more as you see the Day approaching."

So this week we urge you to reconsider your participation in your local church so that you may commit yourselves afresh to fulfill God's purposes there. To help you do this we will focus on: (1) submitting to and supporting the leadership of your local church, (2) committing yourselves to a particular congregation to receive biblical teaching, to worship God, and to enter into a community of prayer, (3) committing yourselves to participate in fellowship with other believers, (4) promising to encourage each other to use your God-given gifts in your local congregation, and (5) committing together to give of your time and treasure to your local church.

Man to Man
with Bill McCartney

God's plan calls for us to take the fruit of what is being produced in our homes into the community. We do this by joining a local church. Being part of a church includes full participation in this expanded family.

There are things God wants to develop in us that will never be fully delivered in our homes. The Lord uses the corporate body to nurture and inspire greater growth. Our children are greatly enhanced when they see other adults who are zealous for God, just like their parents. Therefore, we men need to participate fully in our local church alongside our wives as we lead our entire family into full participation in the church.

Woman to Woman
with Lyndi McCartney

Our families, united in Christ Jesus, are vital to our churches. Our pastors were never meant to carry the whole load of the church. They are to equip the saints for the work of service. That means we need to know our place within the body, to be involved and use our talents and our gifts for kingdom purposes. This starts in our own lives, then spreads to our homes, to our churches, and to our communities. We must keep our priorities straight and maintain balance so we don't become overburdened. In this, Jesus is our guiding light. He knew how to work and how to rest. When we maintain this balance, service is a joy not a burden on you, your family, or anyone in the church.

Some of us get caught up trying to be the woman described in Proverbs 31 and exhaust ourselves. If you are feeling guilty that you do not do enough, that's the enemy tearing you down. Remember that the description given in Proverbs 31 covers one woman's entire lifetime. Be careful not to get so busy with church work that you are fracturing your family. Keep first things first.

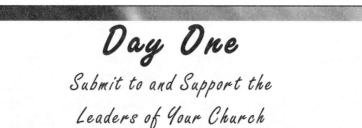

Submit to and Support the
Leaders of Your Church

Purpose

- To consider and comply with God's commands regarding submission to church leadership

- To commit yourselves to be supportive of church leadership

- To get to know and support the mission of your particular congregation

Premise

Hebrews 13:17 clearly states God's standard for submission to church leadership. It says, "Obey your leaders and submit to their authority. They keep watch over you as men who must give an account. Obey them so that their work will be a joy, not a burden, for that would be of no advantage to you." Submit means to yield under the leadership of another. This involves respecting your church leaders' accountability to God and yielding to their decisions, even when they don't do everything the way you want it done. Submission in this way shows respect for the office of church leadership, even if you disagree with a particular decision.

You can demonstrate your submission in many practical ways. You can commit yourselves to not do anything that would cause division or dissension within the congregation. If you have a concern with leadership, take it up with the leaders rather than stirring up popular opinion against them. If you find that there is a particular point of doctrine or church practice that you cannot bear, find a church where you can be supportive of the doctrinal stand and practice. In this way you will be able to fulfill God's command to submit to your spiritual leaders.

The idea of submission also carries with it the idea of lining up behind leaders in military fashion to fulfill their assigned mission. God has given the whole body of Christ an overall mission. This mission includes going into all the world to preach the gospel, making disciples, and teaching them to obey all that Jesus commanded us. It also includes coming into unity as Jesus prayed for his followers in John 17 and includes growing toward purity, since Jesus intends "to purify for himself a people that are his very own, eager to do what is good" (Titus 2:14). It also involves growing in maturity as is stated in Ephesians 4:13, that we all "become mature, attaining to the whole measure of the fullness of Christ."

Within this broad mission of the church as a whole, each congregation has its own emphasis and approach to carrying out God's mission. If you know the mission statement or particular focus of ministry your church leaders are seeking to fulfill, you will be better able to "line up behind them" and "yield under" their leadership.

In addition to submitting to your church leaders, you should also be supporting them with prayer and encouragement. Pastors and church leaders tend to get criticism more than encouragement when they need the prayers and support of their congregation. Paul expressed his own need for the prayers of those under his spiritual leadership when he said, "You help us by your prayers." In 1 Corinthians 16:15–18, Paul pointed out the household of Stephanas, which devoted itself to the service of the saints. He urged the congregation to "submit to such as these and to everyone who joins in the work, and labors at it." He went on to say that such leaders also deserve recognition.

Therefore, part of your involvement together in church should be to pray for your leaders. Pray not only for your pastoral staff but also for the entire staff, volunteer leaders, and their families. You can remind each other to do this any time you are inclined to criticize something happening within the church. When either of you begin to discuss some problem that concerns you, let that be a reminder to immediately pray for the leaders involved. This should be in addition to praying for your church leaders in your regular times of prayer together. You can also help each other by making a commitment not to backbite, gossip about, or slander your leaders—and not to remain in anyone else's conversation that occurs. If you feel compelled to talk about your church leaders, it's best to do so to them directly or on your knees together before the Lord.

Your leaders also deserve recognition and need encouragement. It means so much for church leaders to hear that you appreciate what they do and how they devote themselves to the congregation. Let them know that you are praying for them. Offer encouraging words. Take note of their personal sacrifices and express your appreciation. Once, as a pastor was standing beside Bill McCartney at a Promise Keepers pastor's conference, he was impressed that several men stopped to say that they were praying for Bill, his ministry, and his family. The pastor commented that he wished he would get that same kind of support from his own congregation. Don't let your pastor be in that situation. Make a point of encouraging him or her and the rest of your church leadership regularly.

Practice

1. Identify the mission of your church. If you know the mission, or if there is a published mission statement, write it here. _____

   _____

   _____

   _____

   _____

   If you don't know the mission of your particular church, call the church office and ask someone whether there is a set mission statement. If there is not, make an appointment to meet with someone on the church staff who can explain the particular focus and mission of your congregation.

2. Make a commitment to the Lord and to each other that you will submit to the leadership of your church, support the mission God has given it to accomplish, and not participate in any behavior that tears down, divides, undermines, or otherwise works against what the leaders are seeking to accomplish for the kingdom of God.

   Are you willing to agree to this in your current church? Husband: _____ Wife: _____

If you cannot make this commitment to your current church, discuss whether you need to find another church where you can commit yourselves to submit to the leadership as God requires.

3. Plan to pray for your church leaders. Below make a list of all the leaders of your church that you know by name. Also list areas of ministry where there are leaders that you don't know by name.

If time is short or you don't have all this information, put down what you know now and fill in the rest as you go along.

Known Church Leaders	Ministry Leaders Not Known by Name
Pastor	*Children's Ministry Leaders*
	Youth Ministry Leaders

4. Take some time to pray together for each area of ministry and the leaders involved. If you don't know them by name, pray for the leaders who do particular ministries. For example: You could pray for all the children's ministers, asking God to give them patience, an abundance of love, and wisdom to teach the children.

5. List practical ways you could encourage, show respect for, or express appreciation to some members of your church staff.

⧗ Agree to do one of these things this week. Then do it. Make a point of doing or saying one thing weekly that will be encouraging or helpful to the leaders of your church.

⧗ 6. Agree to turn times of criticism and gossip about church leaders into times of prayer. Plan what you will say to each other or to someone else that will turn negative conversations into constructive prayer. The following is an example; write your own in the space below. If you hear or begin to criticize or gossip about church leaders, you could say instead, "Why don't we pray for them and the problems we see instead of just talking about them. And let's not say anything about them that would offend the Holy Spirit who knows the whole story." What could you say to help turn criticism and gossip about church leaders into prayer?

_____

_____

_____

_____

⧗ Do you agree to do this with each other and not get offended if your mate happens to be the one who catches you falling into a pattern of criticism or gossip? Husband: _____ Wife: _____

Promises

God's Promise to You
"Obey your leaders and submit to their authority. *They keep watch over you as men who must give an account.* Obey them so that their work will be a joy, not a burden, for that would be of no advantage to you" (Heb. 13:17).

Your Promise to Each Other
To agree together to submit to and support the leadership of your local church.

Prayer

Our Father in heaven,

Please forgive us for the ways in which we have disobeyed you by not submitting ourselves to the leaders of our church. We agree today to submit to their leadership, to get to know their mission, and fall in line to accomplish that mission with them. We pray that you will help us become aware of how often we criticize, tear down, gossip, or otherwise undermine the leadership of our church. We pray that the Holy Spirit will convict us whenever we begin to do this and turn our hearts to pray for our leaders instead. Please show us other ways we can support and encourage our leaders as they serve you by serving our congregation.

(Add your own prayers here for the leaders of your church using the lists you made in number 3 of the practice session.) In Jesus' name. Amen!

Day Two
Commit Yourselves to a Church Where You Worship, Pray, and Receive Teaching

Purpose

- To commit yourselves to regular attendance at a church where you gather with others to worship, pray, and receive teaching

Premise

Hebrews 10:25 says, "Let us not give up meeting together, as some are in the habit of doing, but let us encourage one another—and all the more as you see the Day approaching." Regular participation with a body of believers is necessary. It's not only as necessary today as it was in the first century, but it is also something we are to do more and more as we approach the day when Jesus will return for his church.

This verse indicates that meeting with or neglecting to meet with other Christians is a matter of habit. God calls all Christians to be in the habit of going to church to join with other believers for worship, prayer, and instruction in God's Word. Even Jesus gives us this model in his own life. Luke 4:16 tells us, "He went to Nazareth, *where he had been brought up,* and on the Sabbath day he went into the synagogue, *as was his custom.*" Jesus left us this example that we should follow in his steps. Therefore, you should make a habit of meeting with other believers in your church and bringing your children up as part of a congregation of believers.

God has gifted each congregation with people having various abilities. Ephesians 4:11–13 says, "It was he who gave some to be apostles, some to be prophets, some to be evangelists, and some to be pastors and teachers, to prepare God's people for works of service, so that the body of Christ may be built up until we all reach unity in the faith and in the knowledge of the Son of God and become mature, attaining to the whole measure of the fullness of Christ." All Christians are to receive the teaching and ministry of the church leaders so that the body of Christ can be built up, each person growing in the knowledge of Jesus as each becomes a mature believer. Given that the ultimate goal of such teaching is that every believer would attain to the whole measure of the fullness of Christ, the process of learning from God's Word and growing in faith is a lifelong process.

The other benefit of being under the leadership of a good church is that it should protect you from false doctrines. The early Christians submitted themselves to the apostles' teaching, and we must do likewise to avoid being led astray by false teaching. Therefore, make sure you choose a church that believes the Bible to be the inspired and infallible Word of God. This will protect you from error. Paul's letter to Timothy warned against those who would teach or agree to false doctrine. He gave several indicators that would be present if something were amiss. You may want to turn to 1 Timothy 6:3–5 to consider these.

Worship and prayer are spiritual acts that can be done individually or together with other believers. Psalm 95:6–7 calls to us to worship as a group, saying, "Come, let us bow down in worship, let us kneel before the LORD our Maker; for he is our God and we are the people of his pasture, the flock under his care." Even though you can and should worship God individually, there are also times you should come together with others in "the flock" to worship God.

Jesus said that whenever two or three gather in his name, he will be in their midst. When we gather together in Jesus' name to worship and pray, we are truly able to be in tune with the Spirit of God. It was as the early church gathered in worship and prayer that the Holy Spirit came upon them to empower them on the day of Pentecost. It was as the church in Jerusalem met together to pray that Peter was miraculously released from prison by an angel. It was as the church gathered at Antioch to worship with prayer and fasting that the Holy Spirit told them to set apart Paul and Barnabas for their first missionary journey. So, too, you should not neglect worship and prayer as you gather with your local body of believers. And when you are gathered to worship, it should be heartfelt and sincere—in spirit and in truth. For Jesus taught us that "the true worshipers will worship the Father in spirit and truth, for they are the kind of worshipers the Father seeks. God is spirit, and his worshipers must worship in spirit and in truth" (John 4:23–24).

Practice

☒ 1. Answer the following questions: Are you in the habit of regularly gathering with other believers to worship, pray, and receive teaching from God's Word? Husband: _____ Wife: _____

How long have you been in or out of the habit of regularly participating in a church family? Husband: _____ Wife: _____

2. If either of you have ever been in the habit of participating in a regular worship service, but now do not do so, discuss why you think you got out of the habit.

☒ 3. List any current obstacles that hinder you from participating regularly in worshiping, praying, and receiving biblical teaching in your local church.

_____

_____

_____

_____

☒ 4. Consider and discuss these questions. Some of them lend themselves to lengthy discussions. To stay within your time commitment, focus on identifying what keeps you from regular participation in church and what you will do to overcome those obstacles. You can decide now what is right and grow to understand why that may be difficult for you as you go along.

☒ What changes do you need to make so you can regularly participate in meeting with other believers in your local church?

If scheduling is a problem, are there other meetings or Bible studies you could attend?

If you have been hurt by someone or have grown to mistrust people in church for some reason, can you talk this over with someone who can help you get over it?

If you don't like the style of worship, are there other services that allow you to worship in a way that makes you feel more comfortable?

⧗ For each obstacle listed, look for a way to overcome it so you can get back to or maintain the habit of regularly meeting with other believers.

5. Make a list of all the times in the last three months you gathered with other believers in your church fellowship to pray.

Purpose of Prayer	Who Prayed	When?	Where?
_____	_____	_____	_____
_____	_____	_____	_____
_____	_____	_____	_____
_____	_____	_____	_____
_____	_____	_____	_____

This exercise should help you see how active you are in praying with others in your local church. Since prayer is one of the most powerful ways the members of the body of Christ can accomplish their mission and build each other up, you should be praying with other believers in your congregation. If you have not been doing so, list a few issues that you are concerned about related to the mission of your church. Perhaps you are concerned over particular financial or practical issues, or perhaps you are a parent concerned for the spiritual well-being of your children, or you see a particular need that you want to see met through the church, such as developing a vibrant men's ministry or an evangelistic outreach. Choose something you both care about and make plans to pray with others from your church who share this concern. You may have to plan a prayer meeting, or you may ask the people in your small group or Sunday School class to join you in prayer for a particular thing. If you are a parent, you could ask the other parents of kids in your children's classes to join with you to pray for your children and their leaders.

If you cannot think of anything in particular, ask your pastor and church leaders if they would give you a list of their pressing concerns and needs. Then invite several people over after church to pray together for the needs of the leaders of your church.

Promises

God's Promise to You
"For where two or three come together in my name, there am I with them" (Matt. 18:20).

Your Promise to Each Other
To maintain the habit of regularly gathering with other believers to worship, pray, and receive biblical teaching. Also to bring your children up in the habit of regular church participation.

Prayer

Our Father in heaven,

Thank you for calling us into fellowship with you and with each other. Thank you for giving us a country where we are free to worship you in many different ways. Thank you for ready access to good Bible teaching and opportunities to worship you and pray with other believers. Please forgive us to the extent that we have neglected these opportunities. Please forgive us for the times we have fallen out of the habit of getting together with other believers.

Lord, we are willing to commit ourselves to attend a church where we can worship you, pray, and receive good teaching from the Bible. You know the obstacles we face (mention any that you listed earlier). Please help us find ways to overcome all of these obstacles. Please help us bring our children up in a church where they will learn of you and grow to love and serve you. In Jesus' name. Amen!

Purpose

- To understand what Christian fellowship entails

- To commit yourselves to participate in Christian fellowship

Premise

The Bible describes followers of Christ as more than simply those who share similar beliefs. God calls us into his family, his body, signifying that to come into relationship with God requires you to come into relationship with other people. In fact, when Jesus' disciples asked him to teach them how to pray he began with "Our Father," again signifying that when we come into relationship with God the Father, we unavoidably come into relationship with his other children.

The Book of Acts says of the first church, "Every day they continued to meet together in the temple courts. They broke bread in their homes and ate together with glad and sincere hearts, praising God and enjoying the favor of all the people. And the Lord added to their number daily those who were being saved" (2:46–47). They did not only "go to church" to participate in spiritual activities, they also participated in "fellowship" and "the breaking of bread" by coming together in private homes "with glad and sincere hearts."

Coming into fellowship with other believers is meant to be a vital part of the life of any church. God did not simply send down a set of decrees and teachings. He also said that the world would know his teachings were true and that we were disciples of Jesus by the kind of loving relationships we had with each other.

Fellowship may entail getting together with other believers for spiritual activities, but it may also be simply to share a meal and get to know each other. We are to be friends with other believers, build relationships, extend hospitality to each other, invite each other over for dinner. It was in this context that the Lord kept adding to the number daily those who were being saved.

In this day and age when there are so many lonely people, sincere and loving Christian fellowship can be an excellent way to share the love of Jesus with unbelievers. Some churches even plan this into their evangelism goals for the church. In some, couples regularly get together in someone's home for a dinner party. Three couples from a church will get together, and someone will invite another couple who is not yet Christian. The host tells the new couple that the others are from his or her church, so the newcomers don't feel tricked or trapped into an uncomfortable setting. When they all get together, they simply enjoy each other's company. The church-goers don't gang up on the new couple to present the gospel; they simply live out their love and friendship before their new friends. Afterward, the new couple is asked to consider coming to church some time. This not only builds friendships within the local congregation, it has also brought many new families into the church and eventually into God's kingdom.

In addition to meeting together in the large assembly, we need to know and be known among a smaller group of people. Jesus himself ministered among the large crowds but withdrew to a group of twelve and to a smaller circle of three friends with whom he retreated on special occasions. So, too, it will enhance your Christian life to become involved with a smaller group of believers to relate on a more intimate basis. This could be a small group of just men or women, such as a men's small group or women's Bible study group. This could be a group that shares a specific interest or similar struggles—such as in a Christian twelve-step group. Or it could be a few different small groups—some in which you may each be involved individually and perhaps a small group of couples or Christian families with whom you spend time.

Whatever the configuration of your fellowship with other believers, you will need to be committed to conducting yourself according to God's Word. You must study what the Bible says about how we are to relate to each other as Christians and practice conducting yourself as God commands in these relationships. This would include being willing to forgive each other; refusing to slander, gossip, or backbite; doing nothing that would cause another believer to stumble in his or her faith; and treating each other as God's Word says we should.

Christian relationships are not always easy. God calls us to speak the truth in love to each other. He calls us to confront sin and hold each other accountable. He calls us to restore one another in a spirit of gentleness if someone is caught in a sin. He calls us to turn each other back to the truth if we stray in error. He calls us to uphold sound doctrine and correct each other if someone falls prey to false teaching. All of this requires the grace of God, humility, compassion, and the fruit of the Holy Spirit (love, joy, peace, patience, kindness, goodness, faithfulness, gentleness, and self-control).

There will be times when you clash with other Christians, even clash over a point of doctrine or some issue related to the church. There will be times you would rather retreat into isolation, but God doesn't allow for that. He created us to be a body, and there is no part of the body that can cut itself off from the rest and still contribute what it was created to contribute to the working of the whole. Therefore, those who are committed to Christian fellowship must learn to practice intentional reconciliation.

Jesus prayed, "My prayer is not for them alone. I pray also for those who will believe in me through their message, that all of them may be one, Father, just as you are in me and I am in you. May they also be in us so that the world may believe that you have sent me" (John 17:20–21). Jesus prayed for our unity, and he prayed that our unity would cause the world to know that he was truly sent from God.

Truly, unity among believers is not something that can be accomplished by humans alone. Left to ourselves, we will create divisions; we will segregate and separate; we will look down on people who are different from ourselves or who come from a different culture; we will allow our prejudices to keep us apart. Left to ourselves, we will bicker and argue over political or personal issues, we will condemn each other and compare ourselves to each other in ways that put others down to make us feel better about ourselves. Differing social classes will clash, different races will separate from each other, and men and women will set themselves against each other, but this ought not be so in the body of Christ. God's Word declares, "For we were all baptized by one Spirit into one body—whether Jews or Greeks, slave or free—and we were all given the one Spirit to drink" (1 Cor. 12:13); and, "You are all sons of God through faith in Christ Jesus, for all of you who were baptized into Christ have clothed yourselves with Christ. There is neither Jew nor Greek, slave nor free, male nor female, for you are all one in Christ Jesus. If you belong to Christ, then you are Abraham's seed, and heirs according to the promise" (Gal. 3:26–29).

Practice

Where You Are Now?

⧗ Assess how you currently fellowship with other believers by answering the following questions.

1. Which other Christians do you get together with socially? _____
   _____
   _____

2. When was the last time you invited people from your church to join you for social interaction or to develop a potential friendship? _____
   _____
   _____
   _____

3. What small groups are you currently part of that build your fellowship with other Christians? _____
   _____
   _____

4. What groups, "kinds of people," or individuals have you separated yourself from or broken fellowship with in your own mind? (These would be people that you have never had fellowship with and perhaps wouldn't want to fellowship with because of your own prejudice or a previous bad experience with "someone like them." It would also include individuals you have cut off because of some negative attitude, clash, or previous bad experience.) _____
   _____
   _____
   _____
   _____

A Willingness to Develop Fellowship with Other Believers

⧖ Complete the following.

1. Would you be willing to try some of the small groups in your church to find a group you are willing to commit to attending? Husband: _____ Wife: _____

   If so, what small-group opportunities exist that interest you?

   Husband   Wife

   _____   _____

   _____   _____

2. Can you think of anyone, any couple, or another family you would like to get to know better? What activity could you plan to get together with them socially? _____

   _____

   _____

   Make plans to invite them to join you in the near future.

3. Can you think of anyone or any group from whom you have separated yourself? If so, agree to pray together about this, asking God to change your heart so you can practice intentional reconciliation so the body of Christ is not divided.

Promises

God's Promise to You

"How good and pleasant it is when brothers live together in unity!" (Ps. 133:1).

Your Promise to Each Other

To encourage each other to participate in fellowship with other believers.

Prayer

Our Father in heaven,

Please help us learn to live as brothers and sisters in your family. Help us come together in fellowship and learn to treat each other the way the Bible says we should. Lord, please help us find other people within our local church with whom we can fellowship and help us practice hospitality. Show us where we have separated ourselves from other believers. Help us share your desire for unity. Please give us the courage and wisdom to practice intentional reconciliation. Lord, please help us live in such a way that those who watch our lives and relationships will know we are Christians by the love we show for others in your body. In Jesus' name. Amen!

Purpose

- To recognize your God-given gifts and how God wants to use them in the church

- To help each other identify your gifts, talents, skills, and abilities

- To choose to use your God-given gifts to help build up the body of Christ

Premise

Every person has been given gifts by God that he intends to be used in the body of Christ. Read the passage from Ephesians 4:7–16. Christ gave gifts to men and women. He gave "some to be apostles, some to be prophets, some to be evangelists, and some to be pastors and teachers, to prepare God's people for works of service, so that the body of Christ may be built up until we all reach unity in the faith and in the knowledge of the Son of God and become mature, attaining to the whole measure of the fullness of Christ."

While there are some who have ministerial gifts, like that of evangelist or pastor or teacher, all Christians are to be active participants in the body of Christ. We are all to grow up into Christ. "From him the whole body, joined and held together by every supporting ligament, grows and builds itself up in love, as each part does its work." This shows us that even if we don't hold an office of apostle, prophet, evangelist, pastor, or teacher, we still have work to do in the body of Christ. The work we do should be in keeping with our gifts. These can be natural talents, spiritual gifts, or special skills and abilities.

Think about who gave you whatever talents you have. God did. Therefore you can offer those talents back to God for use in his body. Sometimes you won't be able to tell whether a particular ability—such as being well organized—is a natural talent, the spiritual gift of administration, or just a skill you have developed through diligent effort. It really doesn't matter what category you put it in, as long as you put it to good service. God wants you to devote yourself to work in his body as only you can. That means bringing all your gifts, talents, skills, and abilities to him.

In Exodus 31:3–5, the Lord speaks of a man who came to work on building the tabernacle. God said of him, "And I have filled him with the Spirit of God, with skill, ability and knowledge in all kinds of crafts—to make artistic designs for work in gold, silver and bronze, to cut and set stones, to work in wood, and to engage in all kinds of craftsmanship." Here we see that God filled a particular person with "the Spirit of God" and this was in the context of his "skill, ability, and knowledge in all kinds of crafts."

God certainly can use those purely "spiritual gifts" listed in 1 Corinthians 12, but the Holy Spirit can also fill you with skill, ability, and special areas of knowledge and expertise that can be used in God's service. The key point to focus on today is to accept that God has gifted you in ways that you can use to build up the body of Christ.

Ephesians 2:10 says, "For we are God's workmanship, created in Christ Jesus to do good works, which God prepared in advance for us to do." You are God's creative masterpiece, designed with particular gifts so that you are uniquely able to do the work God prepared for you to do. Your responsibility is to recognize what talents and gifts you have, be willing to use them to build up the body of Christ, and offer to use those gifts, beginning in your local church.

Practice

1. On another sheet of paper, each of you list at least five natural talents, spiritual gifts, skills, abilities, and areas of knowledge you recognize in your mate. Think about his or her passions, interests, healthy obsessions, and dreams. You have had the best opportunity of anyone to observe your mate. Use your observations to help identify his or her giftings and natural talents.

2. Go on to make a list of at least five natural talents, spiritual gifts, skills, abilities, and areas of knowledge you recognize in yourself.

⧗ 3. Compare your lists and create a combined list for each of you, drawing together anything listed on either of your private lists. Record those combined lists here.

Husband's Gifts and Abilities

Wife's Gifts and Abilities

_____   _____

_____   _____

_____   _____

_____   _____

_____   _____

⧗ 4. Take turns helping each other think of ways you could volunteer to use your gifts, talents, abilities, knowledge, or skills to build up the body of Christ. For example, if you have mechanical knowledge, could you use it to help a needy family who can't afford to get something fixed? Could you mentor a young person who needs a marketable job skill? If you have artistic talent, could you offer to help decorate the church offices, make sets for a stage production, or create works of art for a craft fair? If you have athletic ability, could you act as a "big brother" for a boy being raised by a single mother? Try to come up with at least one possible way you could help someone else in your church or assist in an ongoing ministry by using your gifts.

Note ways each of you could contribute to building up the body of Christ by using your gifts and abilities.

Husband

Wife

_____   _____

_____   _____

_____   _____

_____   _____

5. After considering your God-given gifts and natural abilities, help each other identify some of the things you are doing that are not in your areas of gifting or ability. (Hint: These will probably be the things you hate to do.) One of the benefits of knowing where you are uniquely gifted is that you can choose to use those gifts and decline opportunities that are not in your area of gifting. List the things you are doing now that you may want to let someone else do because they don't fit with the way God made you.

Things That Don't Use My Gifts:
Husband

Things That Don't Use My Gifts:
Wife

_____   _____

_____   _____

_____   _____

_____   _____

_____   _____

_____   _____

Promises

God's Promise to You

"Give, and it will be given to you. A good measure, pressed down, shaken together and running over, will be poured into your lap. For with the measure you use, it will be measured to you" (Luke 6:38).

Your Promise to Each Other

To encourage each other as you begin to use your gifts to serve others in your church.

Prayer

Our Father in heaven,

Thank you for the many gifts you have given us—for our natural abilities, talents, skills, spiritual gifts, and areas of special knowledge. Lord, please help us discover and appreciate the gifts that we take for granted. Please show us how we can use the gifts you've given us within our church. We ask you to help us see and appreciate your gifts in each other. Please show us needs that we can help to fill. May we be willing to use the gifts you have given us in service to your people. In Jesus' name. Amen!

Day Five
Give of Your Time and Treasure in Your Church

Purpose

- To consider ways you can invest in your local church with time, energy, and money

- To put what you treasure into God's work so your heart will be there also

- To make adjustments in giving of your time, energy, and money to your local church

Premise

Every person on earth has something to give. We all have time, energy, and some form of currency—in varying amounts. Jesus himself had much to say about how we spend our lives. Read Luke 12:15–20 where Jesus warns against greed through the parable of the man who stored up for himself but didn't have the time to enjoy what he had spent his life storing up. Jesus said, "This is how it will be with *anyone who stores up things for himself but is not rich toward God*" (Luke 12:21).

Throughout the Gospels, Jesus doesn't tell his followers that they should not care about wealth, but rather that they should invest their lives in such a way that they can enjoy true and eternal wealth. Jesus' teaching about considering the flowers of the field and the birds of the air is not to say that we should not enjoy sufficient clothing or food, but that we should trust God to provide what we need—and not waste our lives worrying. Jesus insists that when we truly seek first the kingdom of God and his righteousness, God will make sure that all our basic needs are met.

Then Jesus continued, "Do not be afraid, little flock, for your Father has been pleased to give you the kingdom. Sell your possessions and give to the poor. Provide purses for yourselves that will not wear out, a treasure in heaven that will not be exhausted, where no thief comes near and no moth destroys. For where your treasure is, there your heart will be also" (Luke 12:32–34). He said that all Christians can afford to be generous in giving of their lives to others because they have an eternal treasury into which they can invest and from which to draw.

A recent Gallup poll reveals that evangelical believers give an average of 2.8 percent of their income to their local churches. This is not significantly different from the amount non-Christians donate to charity. However, Christian economists project that if all the evangelical believers gave 10 percent of their income to local churches, and those churches used it for charitable causes, all churches would be out of debt and world hunger could be obliterated.

Perhaps one reason Christians are not freely giving to the work of local churches is that they are so bound up in debt themselves that they cannot see their way clear to give to the causes they would like to help. If this is the case for you, consider learning to operate by biblical financial principles that will help you better manage your resources. Your local Christian bookstore has many such resources including those by Larry Burkett, Ron Blue, and Mary Hunt.

The Apostle Paul instructed Timothy, "Command those who are rich in this present world not to be arrogant nor to put their hope in wealth, which is so uncertain, but to put their hope in God, who richly provides us with everything for our enjoyment. Command them to do good, to be rich in good deeds, and to be generous and willing to share. In this way they will lay up treasure for themselves as a firm foundation for the coming age, so that they may take hold of the life that is truly life" (1 Tim. 6:17–19).

It's as if the Bible gives us a higher view of true wealth. If we can truly believe what the Bible says about hoping in God instead of putting our hope in earthly wealth, we will be free to become rich—in good deeds! The focus shifts from what we can get or what we can store up for ourselves to what we have to give. Read the Apostle Paul's account of his own giving to the church in Ephesus in Acts 20:25–35. He gave of his spiritual gifts when he proclaimed the whole will of God (v. 27). He gave of his teaching gift to protect them from those who would distort the truth. He gave from the heart, laboring over them "with tears" (v. 31). He made it clear that he had not "coveted anyone's silver or gold or clothing" (v. 33). Instead, he worked with his hands to supply his own needs. (v. 34). He demonstrated his love for them by doing "hard work" and demonstrated that "by this kind of hard work we must help the weak, remembering the words the Lord Jesus himself said: 'It is more blessed to give than to receive'" (v. 35). So we see here an example of how we are to give of our very lives: our time, our energy—including our emotional energy—and our financial resources.

Practice

The Bible says that wherever your treasure is, there your heart will be also. If you had to judge from where your heart is, where would you say your treasure is? What do you continually think about when your mind wanders? If your heart is not focused on the things of God's kingdom, are you willing to change that by investing more of your life's treasures in things of God? Discuss this with each other.

Everyone has time, energy, and money to spend somewhere in life. If you lack money, give of your time and energy, perhaps by organizing an Angel Tree project with others from your church to collect and distribute Christmas presents to children of inmates. If you lack time, give money and energy or expertise. If you lack energy, consider paying someone who needs a little extra cash to fill the place you wish you had the energy to fill.

Between the two of you, discuss and decide on some way you can make sure you are contributing to the work of God's kingdom through your church.

⧗ Circle any time, energy, or money you have to give.

Wife: I have the following to contribute to my church. Time / Energy / Money

Husband: I have the following to contribute to my church. Time / Energy / Money

List how each of you could use your time, energy, or money to support the work of your church.

Husband	Wife
_____	_____
_____	_____
_____	_____

_____   _____

_____   _____

It's easier to invest in God's work when you truly care about it. It's good to give regularly to your local church's general fund. However, consider ways you would really like to give to the work of God in addition to general giving. How could you give of your time, energy, or money that would bring results you care about? For example, could you head up a project to accomplish a worthy goal, such as raising funds to send the youth pastor to the National Youth Worker's Convention or to help purchase a bus to transport seniors? Find out how your church is contributing to a ministry you care about and decide to give of yourself in some way.

Promises

God's Promise to You

"'Bring the whole tithe into the storehouse, that there may be food in my house. Test me in this,' says the LORD Almighty, 'and see if I will not throw open the floodgates of heaven and pour out so much blessing that you will not have room enough for it. I will prevent pests from devouring your crops, and the vines in your fields will not cast their fruit,' says the LORD Almighty. 'Then all the nations will call you blessed, for yours will be a delightful land,' says the LORD Almighty" (Mal. 3:10–12).

Your Promise to Each Other

To help each other find good ways to store up treasures in heaven.

Prayer

Our Father in heaven,

Please help us see our lives and resources with an eye toward eternity. Please help us not worry about those things that you promise to provide, but rather to seek first your kingdom and your righteousness. Lord, show us how our accounts look on the bankbooks of heaven. Please show us how we can store up for ourselves treasures that cannot be stolen or ruined or lost. Please help us adjust how we spend our time, energy, and money so that we may please you and help support the work of your kingdom. In Jesus' name. Amen!

WEEK EIGHT

Fulfill God's Purpose in Your Community and World Together

Introduction

God is at work accomplishing his purpose for this world, for all creation. He is moving us ever forward toward the fulfillment of his plans that will usher us into eternity. These are exciting days in which we live. This last week's exercises will show you how we can work together to accomplish God's purposes throughout the world today. The exciting part is that it starts right where you are.

Man to Man

with Bill McCartney

Do you know how to define a kingdom heart? My definition is: "This heart wants to participate in what God is doing on a broad scale. This heart gets excited for every church that is experiencing God's power and anointing." Our hope is that you and your wife will not only join together to bring reconciliation in your relationship, your family, and your local church, but also to bring reconciliation throughout God's kingdom and the world.

At Promise Keepers we follow the Eight Principles of Biblical Reconciliation. These are applicable to any relationship—marriage, church splits, cross-racial relationships, cross-denominational relationships; any time people are divided these will help. Perhaps they will help you evaluate your preparedness to be a person who participates in reconciliation wherever you go.

1. *Commitment to Relationship:* Loved by God and adopted into his family, we're called to committed love relationships with our brothers and sisters (Ruth 1:16–17; 1 Cor. 12).

2. *Intentionality:* Experiencing a committed relationship with our brothers and sisters requires purposeful, positive, and planned activities that facilitate reconciliation and right relationships (Eph. 2:14–15).

3. *Sincerity:* We must be willing to be vulnerable and express our feelings, attitudes, differences, and perceptions with the goal of resolution and building trust (John 15:15).

4. *Sensitivity:* We must seek knowledge about our brothers and sisters in order to relate empathetically to people from different denominations, traditions, races, social standings, and cultures (Eph. 4:15–16). A key question to ask is: "Can you help me understand?"

5. *Interdependence:* As we recognize our differences, we also realize that God has placed us as members in the body of Christ where we need and depend on the contributions of each member (2 Cor. 8:12–14).

6. *Sacrifice:* We must be willing to give up an established status or position and accept a lesser position in order to facilitate reconciling relationships (Phil. 2:3–4).

7. *Empowerment:* Through prayer, personal brokenness, repentance, and forgiveness, we remove barriers and are freed to experience the power of the Holy Spirit in reconciling relationships (2 Cor. 8:9).

8. *Call:* We're all called to a ministry of reconciliation, and we're all commanded to be reconciled with our brothers and sisters across racial, cultural, and denominational barriers (2 Cor. 5:17–21; Matt. 22:37–40).

Woman to Woman

with Lyndi McCartney

I have to have order and balance to continuously direct my prayers. First is my personal relationship with Jesus. His love enables me to love my husband and children, care for our home, and be alert to the physical, emotional, and spiritual needs of those within my sphere of responsibility. Through Jesus, our family is unified. We become one building block in our local church. Our church is built by families—block by block. Our church is reaching out to unite with other churches, for we are all the body of Christ. In this process of coming together we have to learn to be reconciled to each other—first in marriage, then in our families, next in our own church, and then with other churches before the world will take us seriously. Together we are reaching out to love, feed, clothe, and reach the lost in our communities and the world.

The beautiful part of this order God set up is when he reveals that together with all the saints we are the bride of Christ Jesus. We started this workbook as one married couple, but it leads us to realize that we are preparing for the most glorious wedding of all—our union with Jesus Christ when he returns for his bride. How awesome that what we do here and now leads to that glorious union!

Day One
Let Your Light Shine Where
You Live to Glorify God

Purpose

- To understand and obey Jesus' command to let your light so shine before men that they will see your good deeds and praise your Father in heaven

- To consider your immediate community and plan ways you can let your light shine together to glorify God

Premise

Jesus said, "You are the light of the world. A city on a hill cannot be hidden. Neither do people light a lamp and put it under a bowl. Instead they put it on its stand, and it gives light to everyone in the house. In the same way, let your light shine before men, that they may see your good deeds and praise your Father in heaven" (Matt. 5:14–16).

In this dark world, people need light, and Jesus announced that individual Christians are the light of the world. The two of you may be the only light of Jesus available to some with whom you interact. Even though you are the light of the world, it is possible that those around you may not see your light. The way you live, the choices you make, and deeds you choose to do or not do will determine whether your light is hidden or held up to give light to everyone who crosses your path: at home, in your neighborhood, with your extended family and friends.

If the two of you want to live your lives sold out to God together, you must make sure that you are allowing your combined light to shine before those who are watching you. There is no great mystery as to what it means to "let your light shine." Jesus made it quite clear that it means to do good deeds others will see and associate with your devotion to God.

In another parable, Jesus gave a more detailed list of these good deeds. After telling a parable about separating sheep from goats, Jesus explained, "Then the King will say to those on his right, 'Come, you who are blessed by my Father; take your inheritance, the kingdom prepared for you since the creation of the world. For I was hungry and you gave me something to eat, I was thirsty and you gave me something to drink, I was a stranger and you invited me in, I needed clothes and you clothed me, I was sick and you looked after me, I was in prison and you came to visit me.' Then the righteous will answer him, 'Lord, when did we see you hungry and feed you, or thirsty and give you something to drink? When did we see you a stranger and invite you in, or needing clothes and clothe you? When did we see you sick or in prison and go to visit you?' The King will reply, 'I tell you the truth, whatever you did for one of the least of these brothers of mine, you did for me'" (Matt. 25:34–40).

It's not only what you do but also the attitude with which you do it that makes your light shine. Philippians 2:14–16a says, "Do everything without complaining or arguing, so that you may become blameless and pure, children of God without fault in a crooked and depraved generation, in which you shine like stars in the universe as you hold out the word of life." Surely, you will want to "hold out the word of life" to those you know, but this verse suggests that first you should make sure that your approach to life—devoid of complaining and arguing (that includes complaining about each other and publicly arguing with each other) should precede holding God's Word out to others. If your relationship is harmonious among those who observe your everyday life, others will be more receptive to hear what you have to say from God's Word. When your conduct toward others is full of light, they will see the contrast between you and the darkness of this world. That will open the way to share God's Word.

Many times people around you have needs that they are ashamed of or afraid to mention for fear of refusal or rejection. Make a point to be on the lookout for such needs as you watch for opportunities to let your light shine in ways that will cause people to notice your kindness, care, and goodness. This world does not show much care for individuals any more—especially individuals who don't seem very important. The Bible says that "God loves a cheerful giver" (2 Cor. 9:7).

If the two of you agree to look for needs that you can fill by giving of yourselves or your material possessions and you do so cheerfully, your light will shine. When it does, God will use you to fulfill his purpose right where you live.

Practice

1. On a separate sheet, make a list together of the places you regularly go and of the people with whom you interact in your everyday lives. Use the following categories to spark your thoughts: home, workplaces, neighborhood (apartment building, block, community center, gymnasium, and so on), holiday gatherings with extended family and friends, school settings (your own or your children's), organizations to which you belong, organizations to which your children belong, people you see on a regular basis in your community (people at the grocery store, cleaners, gas station, doctor's office; your mail carrier, baby-sitters, hairdresser, and so on).

⧗ Ask the Lord to bring to mind anyone within the circle of your everyday lives who the two of you could bless in one or more of the ways Jesus listed. (Below is a list of the kinds of good deeds Jesus mentioned.) List a name or description—such as the new neighbor three doors down—next to each good deed.

⧗ If time is short, focus on one or two categories instead of trying to think of someone for every category right now. Ask the Lord to make you sensitive to situations where you could be of help as they arise.

• Someone who is hungry and in need of something to eat (or in need of someone to invite him or her out for a friendly lunch): _____

_____

• Someone who is thirsty and in need of something to drink (maybe a delivery person working in extreme temperatures): _____

_____

- A stranger in need of an invitation (or someone who needs to be invited into a circle of friends): _____

  _____

- Someone who needs clothes, who you could bless with something you have tucked away, unused, in your closet: _____

  _____

- Someone who is sick, who you could look after, help in practical ways, or just visit: _____

- Someone in prison who you could visit or remember with a letter (or perhaps bless by providing help for his or her children or giving a gift at Christmas through Prison Fellowship): _____

  _____

⌛ 2. Plan together several specific ways you can "let your light so shine" right in your everyday life this week. These do not need to be big events or great deeds, just small deeds done in love and in the name of Jesus. List these possibilities here.

  _____

  _____

  _____

  _____

  _____

  _____

⌛ 3. If there is anything on your list that you can do immediately, do it together.

⌛ 4. Commit yourselves afresh to be on the lookout for opportunities to bless those around you to the glory of God on a regular basis.

⌛ 5. Examine your own relationship with regard to complaining and arguing. On a scale of one to ten, how much do you complain and argue? Zero would be that you never complain or argue. Ten would be that you never cease. The lower the number, the better you are doing at obeying God's Word in this regard.

Husband's self-evaluation: 0 1 2 3 4 5 6 7 8 9 10

Wife's self-evaluation: 0 1 2 3 4 5 6 7 8 9 10

Discuss how your conduct with regard to complaining and arguing either brings glory to your Father in heaven or undermines your good witness to those who know you.

⌛ 6. Make a commitment to each other to try to improve your relationship by curbing your tendency to complain and argue. Ask God to help you both.

Promises

God's Promise to You
Jesus promises that if you live as he described, you will hear him say to you, "Come, you who are blessed by my Father; take your inheritance, the kingdom prepared for you since the creation of the world" (Matt. 25:34).

Your Promises to Each Other
To encourage each other to let your light so shine before others that they will see your good deeds and praise your Father in heaven.

Prayer

Our Father in heaven,

Thank you for making us the light of the world. Help us live so that our light shines to the people who see us in our everyday lives. Lord please keep us aware of the needs around us that people are afraid or ashamed to mention. Please show us how we can regularly bless other people who live and work and play alongside us.

Lord, when we complain and argue, please correct us. Help us to be different from everyone else in this world, so we can shine in contrast to them and people will be drawn to you in this dark world. Lord, may our attitude and actions bring glory to you and prepare hearts so that they will be open as we hold out the word of truth. In Jesus' name. Amen!

Day Two
Let Your Light Shine Where You Work to Glorify God

Purpose

- To consider how you can each let your light shine in your workplace (even if you work at home)

- To encourage, help, and support each other as you develop kingdom goals for your work

Premise

Just as God expressed himself in his work of creation and blessed his children by his work, we are to express ourselves and bless our families through our work. King Solomon, a man gifted with wisdom from God, wrote, "A man can do nothing better than to eat and drink and find satisfaction in his work. This too, I see, is from the hand of God, for without him, who can eat or find enjoyment?" (Eccles. 2:24–25). While it is true that the curse put on humanity after the fall in the garden makes work more of a challenge, God created us to do good works. In Christ our work can be redeemed along with the rest of our lives.

Ephesians 2:10 says, "For we are God's workmanship, created in Christ Jesus to do good works, which God prepared in advance for us to do." God not only honors our work, but he has also prepared work in advance for us to do. Your work should ideally be in keeping with the gifts and natural abilities God gave you. But whatever kind of work you find yourself doing at various times in your life, it is something that God will bless if it is committed to him. Proverbs 16:3 says, "Commit to the LORD whatever you do, and your plans will succeed."

Everyone has work to do, whether paid or unpaid in this world's currency. The Bible emphasizes over and over that whatever work you do, you should be able to do it to the glory of God. Consider these verses: "So whether you eat or drink or whatever you do, do it all for the glory of God" (1 Cor. 10:31). "And whatever you do, whether in word or deed, do it all in the name of the Lord Jesus, giving thanks to God the Father through him" (Col. 3:17). "Whatever you do, work at it with all your heart, as working for the Lord, not for men, since you know that you will receive an inheritance from the Lord as a reward. It is the Lord Christ you are serving. Anyone who does wrong will be repaid for his wrong, and there is no favoritism" (Col. 3:23–25). These all show that whatever we do, we should do it as unto the Lord. God himself will honor our efforts and reward us.

What needs to be considered is whether you are doing *whatever you do* as unto the Lord, devoting you heart to him and doing your very best in a way that is pleasing to God.

There are a few pitfalls commonly experienced with regard to work that can compromise your Christian witness. One is that you may be called upon to do things in your job that are immoral. These moral tests will be closely watched by your co-workers who know that you are Christian. In this case, you need to ask yourselves whether you can do any particular task "as unto the Lord" or "in the name of the Lord." You may want to ask whether you would feel as comfortable doing whatever it is if Jesus were watching—which he is. Or you could ask yourself the phrase popularized by Charles Sheldon, "What would Jesus do?" Then do only what Jesus would do, since you represent Jesus to your co-workers.

Another common pitfall regarding work is the temptation to overwork. In the Ten Commandments, God put a restriction on the amount of work allowed in each week. We are allowed to work six days and to rest one. If you work nonstop, or if your work so consumes your time that you don't spend adequate time with each other, it doesn't matter how important you think your work is—you are violating one of the Ten Commandments. While your co-workers may not care about that, they will notice the negative results that overworking has on your marriage and family relationships. You let your light shine in your work when you keep a godly balance between work and rest, between time spent at work and time spent with your family.

Practice

⧗ Create an assessment of how you need to change to comply with the above verses.

1. Commit your work to the Lord together. Use this as a time when the Holy Spirit can convict you if there are some aspects of your work that cannot be committed to the Lord because they are immoral or contrary to what God says is right and good. List any areas of your work that cannot in good conscience be committed to the Lord. _____

   _____

   _____

   _____

   _____

2. Come up with specific ideas of how you can "let your light shine" so people at work see your good deeds and glorify your Father in heaven. List them here. _____

   _____

   _____

   _____

   _____

3. Ask yourself if you can do your work "in the name of the Lord Jesus, giving thanks to God the Father." If so, take turns thanking God for all that you do at work. Thank him even for the mundane parts of your work that serve some useful purpose.

4. If you cannot thank God for your work, identify what is contrary to what you know God would have you do and list what you need to change to be able to thank God for your work. (You may just need to change your attitude.)

Husband: _____

Wife: _____

5. Ask yourself, "Whatever I do, am I working at it with all my heart, knowing that I am working for the Lord and not for others? Do I work with the awareness that, whatever I do, the Lord will reward me if I do it with a good attitude and with excellence?" Discuss your answers.

6. Consider the people who have treated you unfairly or have otherwise done a wrong that you cannot right. List the wrongs that have gone unsettled here. _____

_____

_____

_____

_____

_____

⧗ Present these to God in prayer, asking him to right the wrongs and thanking him because he doesn't play favorites. Forgive whoever you blame and leave it with the Lord. That alone will change your countenance in a way that will cause your light to shine.

Promises

God's Promise to you

"Serve wholeheartedly, as if you were serving the Lord, not men, because you know that the Lord will reward everyone for whatever good he does, whether he is slave or free" (Eph. 6:7–8).

Your Promise to Each Other

To remind each other to do everything as unto the Lord. To encourage each other to work heartily and with excellence.

Prayer

Our Father in heaven,

Thank you for the satisfaction that comes from work well done. Thank you that whatever we do is valued by you and will be rewarded by you if we do it as unto you. Lord, please help us approach our work with devotion, giving it our best efforts. We pray that our light will shine in our work and our workplaces so that those around us will see your light through us. Please help us to turn over to you those wrongs that we cannot right at work and to conduct ourselves with excellence, truthfulness, and whole-hearted devotion to the work you have given us to do. In Jesus' name. Amen!

Day Three
Work Together to Fulfill the Great Commission

Purpose

- To consider how you can obey the Great Commission Jesus gave to all believers

- To consider the stages of your outreach, starting right where you live, reaching out to your surrounding community, and considering how you can help take the gospel message to the uttermost parts of the world

- To commit yourselves afresh to sharing the good news of Jesus Christ in specific ways and begin doing it

Premise

Mark's Gospel records what happened when the Lord appeared to his disciples after his resurrection. "He said to them, 'Go into all the world and preach the good news to all creation. Whoever believes and is baptized will be saved, but whoever does not believe will be condemned'" (16:15–16). This has come to be known as the Great Commission. It is to be a life mission for every Christian. As a married couple, it should also be a primary co-mission that the two of you agree to pursue together.

Mark's Gospel goes on to say, "After the Lord Jesus had spoken to them, he was taken up into heaven and he sat at the right hand of God. Then the disciples went out and preached everywhere, and the Lord worked with them and confirmed his word by the signs that accompanied it" (16:19–20).

Jesus is the same yesterday, today, and forever. Just as he worked with the first-century disciples and confirmed his word through them, he is eager to do the same through the two of you. However, it is your choice as to whether you will receive and respond to his Great Commission. The first disciples went out and preached everywhere. Are you willing to accept the mission to do likewise in keeping with your personality and spiritual gifting? The gospel can be spread in many ways. What's yours?

Matthew records this account of what took place after Jesus was raised from the dead, "Then the eleven disciples went to Galilee, to the mountain where Jesus had told them to go. When they saw him, they worshiped him; but some doubted. Then Jesus came to them and said, 'All authority in heaven and on earth has been given to me. Therefore go and make disciples of all nations, baptizing them in the name of the Father and of the Son and of the Holy Spirit, and teaching them to obey everything I have commanded you. And surely I am with you always, to the very end of the age'" (Matt. 28:16–20).

Here we see an added dimension to our commission from Jesus. We are to participate in making disciples, baptizing them and teaching them to obey all Jesus commanded us. But we also have the promise that Jesus will work with us in this—"to the very end of the age." This last phrase shows us that this commission continues on to believers in all generations—that includes the two of you. It also means that Jesus stands ready to work with you and be with you as you do your part to fulfill the Great Commission.

Luke wrote not only his Gospel, but also the Acts of the Apostles, wherein he writes of Jesus, "After his suffering, he showed himself to these men and gave many convincing proofs that he was alive. He appeared to them over a period of forty days and spoke about the kingdom of God. On one occasion, while he was eating with them, he gave them this command: 'Do not leave Jerusalem, but wait for the gift my Father promised, which you have heard me speak about. For John baptized with water, but in a few days you will be baptized with the Holy Spirit.' So when they met together, they asked him, 'Lord, are you at this time going to restore the kingdom to Israel?' He said to them: 'It is not for you to know the times or dates the Father has set by his own authority. But you will receive power when the Holy Spirit comes on you; and you will be my witnesses in Jerusalem, and in all Judea and Samaria, and to the ends of the earth'" (Acts 1:3–8).

Notice that even the apostles and disciples who walked with Jesus on earth were not spiritual enough to go out in their own strength. They had to wait until the power of the Holy Spirit came on them. Then they became witnesses of Jesus Christ, demonstrating his power as he worked with them. Neither are we equipped to go out and be witnesses of Jesus in our own strength. We are not to attempt to fulfill any part of the Great Commission until we receive the power of the Holy Spirit so that we can be his witnesses.

There are differing opinions about the empowering of the Holy Spirit that have become points of contention and divided Christians. We have no desire to spark such division. Rather, we urge you to seek God afresh for the power of the Holy Spirit you will need to truly be living witnesses for Jesus.

The first-century disciples received this message while living in Jerusalem. Therefore, their mission was to begin at home. Then it was to spread into Judea and Samaria, their surrounding region, including their fellow Jews, with whom they felt comfortable, and the racially mixed Samaritans, whom they despised because of racial and religious biases. They were also to reach out beyond their home territory to break down the walls of racism and sectarianism that separated them from those in the outlying regions, then spread the gospel to the ends of the earth.

We can also follow their pattern. We have already looked at ways you can let your light shine at home and where you work. This is where your communication of the gospel should begin too. Then you are to find ways—as you are led by the Holy Spirit—to go beyond your home base, to your surrounding region, to reach people you already feel comfortable with as well as those who live across the racial, sectarian, and territorial boundaries in your lives. Finally you are to find ways to help take the gospel to the very ends of the earth—which is tremendously exciting, given the age in which we live.

Practice

⧗ If time is short, focus on the basics of sharing the gospel given in steps 1 through 4.

1. Identify how you have already prepared yourselves to share the gospel. What have you done to be ready to do any of the following: share your personal testimony, present a simple explanation of how to become a

Christian (perhaps using a tract or outline), give logical reasons for your faith in the Bible and the claims of Jesus Christ, reach out in friendship to non-Christians in hopes of inviting them to church or into relationship with your Christian friends, perform acts of kindness in Jesus' name, pray for the salvation of specific people. _____

_____

2. Are you utilizing the power of the Holy Spirit so you can be witnesses of Jesus wherever you go? If you are not sure, ask God to give you the power you will need to share the gospel. Ask him to help you not to quench the Spirit's fire. Also ask the Holy Spirit to direct you as you seek to fulfill the Great Commission together.

3. Rehearse with each other your personal testimony of what Jesus has done in your life. Speak of what your life was like before you met Jesus as your Savior, how you came to repent and receive Jesus Christ, how Jesus has changed your life and your outlook on life.

4. If you are uncertain how to lead others to receive Jesus as their Savior, plan to get a good resource to prepare you to do so. These are available through your local Christian bookstore. Or check with the leadership of your church for resources or classes.

⧗ The following considerations of your Great Commission to go to your "Jerusalem," your "Judea and Samaria," and to the "uttermost parts of the earth" supply questions that can become the basis for ongoing discussions and decisions. If your time today is running short, pick one item in each section to help you clarify your understanding of God's greater mission for your life. You can come back and go into greater detail later.

Consider Your "Jerusalem" Mission
How can the two of you contribute to fulfilling the Great Commission where you live and work everyday? What can you do directly? Who do you know who needs to receive Jesus as Savior? Make a prayer list of five people in your "Jerusalem" who you will commit yourself to praying for and stand prepared to

share with them if God gives you the opportunity. The five people within our reach whose salvation we will continually pray for are:

1. _____

2. _____

3. _____

4. _____

5. _____

Consider Your "Judea and Samaria" Mission

How can the two of you contribute to fulfilling the Great Commission in your local region? This includes your geographic region, such as your city, county, or state. Are there evangelistic activities happening on a larger scale that you could participate in or help to finance? What evangelistic efforts are being planned or conducted by your local church or denomination that you could participate in or help to finance? What evangelistic organizations are at work in your region? You can call your local Christian radio station, key churches in your area, Promise Keeper representatives in your region, or such para-church groups that target specific segments of the population as Youth for Christ or Campus Life for suggestions. List several options you have for participating in the evangelistic efforts going on in your region. _____

_____

_____

_____

_____

_____

Reaching your "Judea and Samaria" also includes reaching out beyond the racial and sectarian divisions that may be a part of your culture. The Jews, to whom the original commission was given, hated the Samaritans. Their culture was so filled with racial tension that most Jews would travel great distances out of their way to avoid passing through Samaria. And yet Jesus specifically commanded them to go where he knew they didn't want to go. Are you willing to meet with believers of other races and denominations in vital prayer partnerships to seek to reach your area for Christ as representatives of the larger body of Christ? List any ways you could reach across the boundary of your own biases to join other Christians in sharing the gospel with groups with whom you don't feel comfortable. _____

_____

_____

_____

_____

Consider Your Mission to Reach the Ends of the Earth with the Gospel

How can the two of you contribute to fulfilling the Great Commission throughout the world? There are many fine efforts under way to take the gospel to every part of the world and to every unreached person. Are you willing to do something to help spread the gospel to the ends of the earth? What are you already doing? Here are just a few of the options available to us in the age in which we live: helping to translate the Holy Bible into every language on the globe through organizations like the Wycliff Bible Translators; supporting worldwide evangelistic efforts like those of the Billy Graham Evangelistic Association; going on a short-term mission trip through your local church, denomination, or a missions organization; supporting a child through the efforts of Christian Relief Organizations such as World Vision or Compassion International; using or supporting broadcast media to send the gospel message to every part of the world through Christian television programming, Christian radio, or the Internet. The possibilities are beyond what Christians in any other generation could even imagine. What are you doing to make the most of these opportunities? Is there a particular country or people who are dear to your heart? What ministries that take the gospel to the ends of the earth do you have confidence in? List those ministries here.

_____

_____

_____

⌛ What will the two of you do to participate in the completion of the Great Commission? Discuss this question, then write your commitment to do this together here: _____

_____

_____

_____

_____

_____

Promises

God's Promise to You

"Jesus came to them and said, 'All authority in heaven and on earth has been given to me. Therefore go and make disciples of all nations, baptizing them in the name of the Father and of the Son and of the Holy Spirit, and teaching them to obey everything I have commanded you. And surely I am with you always, to the very end of the age'" (Matt. 28:18–20).

Your Promise to Each Other

To agree and work together to help fulfill the Great Commission.

Prayer

Our Father in heaven,

Thank you for the privilege of being your witnesses on this earth. Thank you for sending your Holy Spirit to empower us so that we could become your witnesses. Lord we are willing to go as you have told us to go, to proclaim your good news, and to help make disciples. Please show us what we can do in our own daily surroundings. Please show us who needs to hear about your love for them and give us the opportunity to share with them. Please give us boldness to open our mouths to speak your word. Help us prepare ourselves so we can give an answer for the hope that is within us. We also pray that you show us ways to reach out and share the gospel in our surrounding region. Show us how to get beyond the racial biases and sectarian views that have separated us from Christians of different races and denominations. Please help us unite together in vital prayer partnership. Please help us combine our efforts, contacts, talents, spiritual gifts, and resources to spread the gospel. Lord, show us how we can contribute to the work of those who are taking the gospel to the ends of the earth. Help us reassess our giving so that we can help get your message and ministry out to everyone before you return. In Jesus' name. Amen!

Day Four
Come Together with Other Christians in One Body

Purpose

- To review Jesus' prayer that we would be one with other Christians

- To consider the need for intentional reconciliation wherever there is division in the body of Christ

- To consider how you can join with other Christians in one body without compromising the distinctiveness of your particular denomination

Premise

Our unity as Christians was of the utmost importance to the Lord Jesus. When he prayed for his disciples just before he died, unity was at the heart of his desire for his people.

Yet there are many sources of division in the body of Christ, division between you and other individual Christians in your personal relationships, divisions and factions within the local church, divisions between races, denominational barriers that set one Christian group against another, divisions between rich and poor, male and female, those who hold power and those who have been oppressed.

The Apostle Paul wrote, "May the God who gives endurance and encouragement give you a spirit of unity among yourselves as you follow Christ Jesus, so that with one heart and mouth you may glorify the God and Father of our Lord Jesus Christ. Accept one another, then, just as Christ accepted you, in order to bring praise to God" (Rom. 15:5–7). Here we see that Paul prayed for God to give them a spirit of unity to follow Christ Jesus with one heart and mouth. The result would be that the Christians who lived in such unity would "glorify the God and Father of our Lord Jesus Christ."

On a practical note, Paul told the Ephesian Christians, "Be completely humble and gentle; be patient, bearing with one another in love. Make every effort to keep the unity of the Spirit through the bond of peace." It not only takes God's help, and prayer, but all Christians must also "make every effort to keep the unity" in the body of Christ. It takes sustained effort.

Unity is the result of choosing to love and forgive each other and to let the peace of Christ rule in our hearts. "Bear with each other and forgive whatever grievances you may have against one another. Forgive as the Lord forgave you. And over all these virtues put on love, which binds them all together in perfect unity. Let the peace of Christ rule in your hearts, since as members of one body you were called to peace. And be thankful" (Col. 3:13–15).

When Jesus commanded his disciples to love each other, he had a greater purpose in mind. He said, "A new command I give you: Love one another. As I have loved you, so you must love one another. By this all men will know that you are my disciples, if you love one another" (John 13:34–35). The distinguishing mark that would prove to the world that we are Jesus' disciples is not identical doctrinal statements or agreed-upon mission statements but our love for each other. This is why it is imperative that we come together as one body, loving each other purely on the basis of our common bond in Christ Jesus. He has loved every one of his disciples—regardless of denominational affiliation or lack thereof, regardless of skin color or racial heritage, regardless of whether we are rich or poor, male or female. He commands us to love each other as he has loved us.

When we do, and when we come together to worship our Lord and Savior Jesus Christ as one body, the world will see the glory of God. Then others will know that we are truly his disciples.

Practice

⌛ Read the prayer Jesus prayed for us (see boxed text). As you read, look for the answers to these questions.

⌛ As a time saver, you may want to answer these questions aloud rather than write them in your workbook. One of you can record your answers later if you like.

- How many times does Jesus pray for unity or for his followers to be one (see bold)? _____

- To whom does this prayer apply? _____

- According to Jesus, what will let the world know that the Father sent him and that the Father loves his followers as he loved Jesus? _____

  _____

- In addition to unity, what did Jesus ask for his followers (see italics)?

  _____

  _____

  _____

  _____

  _____

  _____

Jesus' Prayer for Us

After Jesus said this, he looked toward heaven and prayed: "Father, the time has come. Glorify your Son, that your Son may glorify you. For you granted him authority over all people that he might give eternal life to all those you have given him. Now this is eternal life: that they may know you, the only true God, and Jesus Christ, whom you have sent. I have brought you glory on earth by completing the work you gave me to do. And now, Father, glorify me in your presence with the glory I had with you before the world began.

"I have revealed you to those whom you gave me out of the world. They were yours; you gave them to me and they have obeyed your word. Now they know that everything you have given me comes from you. For I gave them the words you gave me and they accepted them. They knew with certainty that I came from you, and they believed that you sent me. I pray for them. I am not praying for the world, but for those you have given me, for they are yours. All I have is yours, and all you have is mine. And glory has come to me through them. I will remain in the world no longer, but they are still in the world, and I am coming to you.

Holy Father, *protect them by the power of your name*—the name you gave me—so **that they may be one as we are one.** While I was with them, I protected them and kept them safe by that name you gave me. None has been lost except the one doomed to destruction so that Scripture would be fulfilled.

"I am coming to you now, but I say these things while I am still in the world, so that they may have the full measure of my joy within them. I have given them your word and the world has hated them, for they are not of the world any more than I am of the world. *My prayer is not that you take them out of the world but that you protect them from the evil one.* They are not of the world, even as I am not of it. *Sanctify them by the truth;* your word is truth. As you sent me into the world, I have sent them into the world. For them I sanctify myself, that they too may be truly sanctified.

"My prayer is not for them alone. I pray also for those who will believe in me through their message, **that all of them may be one, Father, just as you are in me and I am in you.** May they also be in us so that the world may believe that you have sent me. I have given them the glory that you gave me, **that they may be one as we are one:** I in them and you in me. **May they be brought to complete unity** to let the world know that you sent me and have loved them even as you have loved me.

"*Father, I want those you have given me to be with me where I am, and to see my glory, the glory you have given me because you loved me before the creation of the world.*

"Righteous Father, though the world does not know you, I know you, and they know that you have sent me. I have made you known to them, and will continue to make you known in order *that the love you have for me may be in them and that I myself may be in them.*" (John 17:1–26)

⧖ The idea of the body of Christ being one and operating in unity can seem more conceptual than practical. We recommend four specific things you can do to help bring about unity in the body of Christ.

1. Regularly pray for unity in the whole body of Christ around the world.

2. Focus on the essentials of faith that we share with all those who love and serve Jesus Christ, and for whom the Holy Bible is Holy Scripture, the inspired Word of God.

3. Practice intentional reconciliation. Whenever you notice a division between you and another Christian, or between a Christian group you are part of and another group of Christians, take the initiative to reconcile.

4. Practice vital prayer partnerships with Christians beyond your immediate group of Christian friends or your local church. This can be done by gathering to pray for common concerns with Christians in your larger community of faith.

⧗ Jesus is coming back for his bride. His prayer for us is that we will be one, sanctified by his truth and eagerly awaiting his return. What will the two of you do to help bring such unity in the body of Christ? Discuss this and come up with one specific action you will take in each of the four areas just cited.

1. When will you regularly pray for unity in the whole body of Christ around the world? _____

2. How will you focus on the essentials of faith that you share with all Christians? _____

   _____

   _____

   _____

   _____

3. How will you practice intentional reconciliation? _____

   _____

   _____

With whom do you need reconciliation in your circle of Christian friends?

_____

_____

How can you help to bring reconciliation between groups of divided Christians? _____

_____

_____

_____

4. How can you practice vital prayer partnerships with Christians beyond your immediate group? (For example: Are there any city- or state-wide prayer meetings in which you could participate? Could you invite the parents from several churches in your area to get together to pray for the youth of your area? Could you agree with all the men or women of your area to pray together as men and women of God? Could you participate in prayer between Christians of various groups for the purpose of evangelism or to specifically pray for unity in the whole body of Christ?) What can you do? _____

_____

_____

Promises

God's Promise to You

"As high priest that year he prophesied that Jesus would die for the Jewish nation, and not only for that nation but also for the scattered children of God, to bring them together and make them one" (John 11:51–52).

Your Promise to Each Other

To work together to create unity within the larger body of Christ and to bring reconciliation wherever you see it needed.

Prayer

Our Father in heaven,

The last thing Jesus prayed for us before his death was that we would be one. Can we pray for any less? Lord, it seems that we do not truly understand the great importance you have put on unity. Please open our hearts to understand. Please cause us to yearn for, pray for, and work for unity as much as Jesus did.

Lord, we ask specifically that you would show us any ways we have caused division in your body and help us to repent of this. Please show us what we can now do to practice intentional reconciliation. Show us how we can partner with other Christians in the larger body of Christ so that we may demonstrate unity to the watching world. Lord, we want the world to know that we are your disciples, therefore help us to truly love every other person as you have loved us. Please keep us from slandering, gossiping about, or otherwise maligning any other person. In Jesus' name. Amen!

Day Five

Continue to Live Sold Out to God Together

Purpose

- To commit yourselves to continue living sold out to God together

- To plan how you can maintain your spiritual connection

- To understand how you can use an ongoing journal to keep track of your spiritual partnership and what God is accomplishing through the two of you

Premise

Hopefully, this experience of devoting yourselves afresh to the Lord together has been a boost to your faith and spiritual effectiveness. However, we have merely touched on vital aspects of your spiritual lives that God desires to deepen in your relationship with each other and with him. Therefore, we hope and pray that the end of this eight-week workbook will mark the beginning of a new way of life shared by the two of you. We hope that you will continue to:

- Seek first the kingdom of God and his righteousness together

- Worship God together on a regular basis, both when it's just the two of you and when you worship in the assembly of believers

- Pray together every day and during special seasons of prayer for specific purposes

- Get into God's Word together and get God's Word into you on a regular basis

- Continually engage in spiritual warfare together and on each other's behalf

- Continually help each other fulfill God's purposes for your family

- Continually help and encourage each other to fulfill God's purposes within your local church

- Continually help each other do your part to fulfill God's purposes within your community and the world

These things will not happen on their own. We live in a world where the momentum of life goes contrary to the things of God's kingdom. Therefore, if you are going to continue to live sold out to God together, you will have to commit yourselves to continue doing the things that you have learned and begun to do in this workbook. Each week of exercises is only a starting place. You can follow up in your own church, with a group of like-minded couples, within your group of like-minded men or women, or just the two of you agreeing together to continue what you have begun.

We have solid advice about continuing wholeheartedly in the things of God in the Scripture. King Solomon prayed, "O LORD, God of Israel, there is no God like you in heaven above or on earth below—you who keep your covenant of love with your servants who *continue* wholeheartedly in your way" (1 Kings 8:23).

The Apostle Paul instructed the Philippian Christians saying, "Therefore, my dear friends, as you have always obeyed—not only in my presence, but now much more in my absence—*continue* to work out your salvation with fear and trembling, for it is God who works in you to will and to act according to his good purpose" (Phil. 2:12–13).

All that you have done together in this workbook could be called "working out" your salvation, as you have applied it in your everyday lives. We have directed you to do those things that are basic to Christian growth and that are according to God's good purpose as revealed in the Bible. But doing it once is not enough. God wants you to continue to work out what he has worked into you—your calling, gifting, and the unique love relationship you share as husband and wife.

We are told that our spiritual life is a continual process of growth throughout the seasons of life. Paul wrote, "So then, just as you received Christ Jesus as Lord, *continue* to live in him, rooted and built up in him, strengthened in the faith as you were taught, and overflowing with thankfulness" (Col. 2:6–7).

We encourage you to do this and with good reason. There is more at stake here than just your individual spiritual lives, or even your testimony as a married couple whose union is meant to be a living example of Christ's love for the church. We, as fellow Christians, are all aiming toward becoming one body, the bride of Christ, eagerly awaiting his return so that we can be wed to him. This is why your continuance matters. The Apostle John wrote, "And now, dear children, *continue in him,* so that when he appears we may be confident and unashamed before him at his coming" (1 John 2:28).

Practice

Here is how you can agree and plan to continue living sold out to God together:

1. Maintain your spiritual connection. You have begun sharing spiritual practices that you may not have shared before. Incorporate shared worship, prayer, study of God's Word, and spiritual warfare into your daily lives. (Remember that the divorce rate drops from 1 in 2 to 1 in 1,052 for couples who pray together every night.)

2. Use a practical tool to keep track of your shared prayer requests, expressions of gratitude to God and each other, and the spiritual battles you are fighting together and on each other's behalf. Record victories in these spiritual battles and verses of Scripture that you can memorize to encourage each other and claim as God's promises to you. Be sure to focus on the godly dreams and desires each of you has; write these down as goals and as the subject of prayer on each other's behalf. Keep track of God's purpose for your family and how you are working together to fulfill it during each season of your lives. Keep track of God's purpose for your local church, your church's mission statement, and how you are

contributing to the accomplishment of that mission. Keep track of how you are working together to become one with the larger body of Christ and helping to fulfill the Great Commission. When you write these down—whether in a place devoted to keeping track of remaining sold out to God together or incorporated into your personal planner—you will be able to help each other continue fulfilling God's purposes for your lives.

3. Make yourselves accountable to each other and to others in the body of Christ. Share any new or renewed commitments regarding your spiritual lives with each other and those to whom you hold yourselves accountable in the body of Christ. Let them know that you want to continue doing these things and ask them to check in with you to see how you are doing at regular intervals (monthly, quarterly, or annually).

4. Commit yourselves to continue practicing ways to remain sold out to God together, and give yourself a checkup. To do so, flip through this workbook and make a list of the spiritual exercises and disciplines that you want to continue to practice together. Seal it in an envelope addressed to yourselves and give it to a mutual friend (who tends to be well organized). Ask this friend to mail this list back to you in three months. This will serve as a reminder to help you see how well you are doing in continuing to live sold out to God together.

Promises

God's Promise to You
"He who began a good work in you will carry it on to completion until the day of Christ Jesus" (Phil. 1:6b).

Your Promise to Each Other
To encourage each other to continue to live sold out to God together. To promise that when either of you asks to continue something you've begun to do in this workbook, you will cooperate with enthusiasm.

Prayer

Our Father in heaven,

You know how prone we are to drift away from you and each other. Please help us help each other not to do so. You have given us such a gift in the form of a Christian mate. Please help us to make the most of this marriage partnership here on earth so that we can live to glorify you. Please help us continue to live sold out together. In Jesus' name. Amen!

Appendix A
Using Sold Out Two-Gether as a Resource for Men's Small Groups

Many men's small groups emphasize the importance of men connecting spiritually with their wives while becoming more responsible husbands, fathers, and participants in their churches. *Sold Out Two-Gether* encourages all of these things.

Following are suggestions for how you can incorporate this workbook into the overall experience of spiritual growth for your married men.

Ongoing Men's Small Groups

In an ongoing men's small group in which all participants are married, ask members to agree to go through the workbook with their wives. In a men's small group that combines married and single men, the married men may wish to meet at another time to discuss together their experience of using this workbook with their wives.

Your small group meetings can focus on the theme each man has been working on with his wife that week. A suggested format for such meetings would include:

- Opening prayer.

- Reading a selected passage of the premise or asking each man to share what passages of the premise he benefited from most.

- Reading a selected passage of Scripture from that week's practice material.

- Reflecting on the meaning of the Scripture readings.

- Sharing regarding the growth each man experienced in light of the goal for the week. (Be careful not to compare one man's spiritual "attainment" to any one else's. Rather focus on how each man grew to some degree.)

- Sharing regarding what the men found most challenging during the week's exercises. (Be sure not to allow men to denigrate their wives before the other men.)

- Gathering prayer requests that are in keeping with the goal for the week.

- Reviewing the theme for the upcoming week and discussing areas of concern the men can pray about in advance. These would include any areas of hesitation or confusion.

- Closing in prayer. Ask each man to pray for blessing on his wife and their shared experience of using this workbook; pray the requests gathered earlier; pray over areas of concern related to the theme of the coming week.

Appendix B
Using Sold Out Two-Gether as a Resource for Women's Small Groups

Many women's small groups emphasize the importance of women connecting spiritually with their husbands while being good wives, mothers, and participants in their churches. *Sold Out Two-Gether* encourages all of these things.

Following are suggestions for how you can incorporate this workbook into the overall experience of spiritual growth for your married women.

Ongoing Women's Small Groups

In an ongoing women's small group in which all participants are married, ask members to agree to go through the workbook with their husbands. In a women's small group that combines married and single women, the married women may wish to meet at another time to discuss together their experience of using this workbook with their husbands.

Your small group meetings can focus on the theme each woman has been working on with her husband that week. A suggested format for such meetings would include:

- Opening prayer.

- Reading a selected passage of the premise or asking each woman to share what passages of the premise she benefited from most.

- Reading a selected passage of Scripture from that week's practice material.

- Reflecting on the meaning of the Scripture readings.

- Sharing regarding the growth each woman experienced in light of the goal for the week. (Be careful not to compare one woman's spiritual "attainment" to any one else's. Rather focus on how each woman grew to some degree.)

- Sharing regarding what the women found most challenging during the week's exercises. (Be sure not to allow women to denigrate their husbands before the other women.)

- Gathering prayer requests that are in keeping with the goal for the week.

- Reviewing the theme for the upcoming week and discussing areas of concern the women can pray about in advance. These would include any areas of hesitation or confusion.

- Closing in prayer. Ask each woman to pray for blessing on her husband and their shared experience of using this workbook; pray the requests gathered earlier; pray over areas of concern related to the theme of the coming week.

Appendix C
Using Sold Out Two-Gether as a Resource for Couple's Small Groups, Marriage Ministries, and Premarital Ministries

Sold Out Two-Gether can be easily adapted to the various marriage-related ministries of your church. You can choose from any of the following applications:

- Suggest the workbook to couples in your church for individual study.

- Use the workbook within your couple's ministries and adapt your regular ministry meetings around the weekly themes.

- Suggest this resource in marriage ministry or marriage counseling settings. Couples who are going through particular marital problems can only be helped by focusing together on the things of God.

- Use this workbook as part of your premarital program. While it is no substitute for premarital counseling, it can allow the potential marriage partners to go out for what one fiancée called a "spiritual test drive." Recognize that the material in the family section should be thought of as what the couple would be committing themselves to in the future. And they would have to postpone the sexual intimacy suggested in week six, day two until after the wedding!

Start Couple's Small Groups Using *Sold Out Two-Gether*

- Plan a start date for the eight-week session, so everyone will have the sense of working on this together.

- Hold sign-ups for couples (gather groups of four to eight couples). Allow each group to choose the time that works best for meeting each week.

- Appoint small-group leaders deemed responsible according to your church leadership. Or allow each group to designate a leader or facilitator.

- Organize a special dinner or prayer meeting to prepare all participants for the spiritual endeavor they are embarking on.

- Have each group meet weekly. Participants may wish to gather for dinner and to discuss the week's experiences together then break into same-gender groups for the meetings. Follow the guidelines for men's and women's small groups.

- Conclude the eight-week study with a couple's retreat or a special dinner or meeting where there can be open sharing of the spiritual progress made. You can also focus as a church on how you can work together to continue fulfilling God's purposes in your marriages, families, local church, larger body of Christ, and the world. Follow this with prayer and an agreement to implement any of the ministry ideas and commitments that came about during the eight weeks.

Create Men's and Women's Small Groups from Couple's Groups

If your church has an active couple's ministry but would like to develop more men's and women's small groups, this is one way you can launch new groups. After meeting for eight weeks to discuss this workbook, each group of men and women may wish to continue meeting.

If several couples go through the workbook together, they may want to finish up with a retreat to celebrate and solidify what they have experienced in becoming sold out to God together. This can be an informal retreat planned by several couples or one sponsored by a church or Bible study group.

Here are some suggestions for a follow-up couple's retreat:

- Make sure the facilities are comfortable and allow for larger meetings and private times for couples.

- Ask someone to organize the weekend so that it flows smoothly. (Here's a great chance for someone who discovered gifts of organization and administration!)

- Agree on the flow of the weekend before you set out together. You can make it a light-hearted retreat with some sharing and praying about what you experienced, along with lots of free time. Or you can choose to create a spiritually intense weekend with planned times to seek God first, worship, pray, get into God's Word, practice spiritual warfare, and advance God's purposes in family, church, and the world. Either is fine as long as everyone is comfortable with it.

- Allow time to gather as a group and time to separate as couples. Have some planned meetings and some free time. Allow time for worship, prayer, and fellowship with God as well as time for fellowship with one another in an informal way.

- Keep the focus on the themes of each week and on positive growth.

Appendix E
Using Sold Out Two-Gether to Help Church Leaders Accomplish the Purposes of God in Their Church

In addition to the help *Sold Out Two-Gether* can provide in areas of marriage ministry, it urges men and women to become actively involved in fulfilling God's purposes for the local church, the larger body of Christ, and our mission as Christians in fulfilling the Great Commission.

If you are a church leader, prayerfully consider how you might help those in your congregation fit their desire to fulfill God's purpose in the local church into the mission God has given you. There are several sections (week six, day four; all of weeks seven and eight) where couples are urged to connect with the church to accomplish God's purposes. Take the initiative. Have answers ready for the questions they will ask. Be prepared to incorporate them into your church's ministry. Be open to the ideas this experience may generate within your church family to expand ministry.

You may want to organize with small group meetings and plan church activities to coincide with the weeks that the small groups will be considering their part in fulfilling God's purposes within your church, within your region, and together with other Christians to the uttermost parts of the earth.